Table of Contents

I.   **Executive Summary** _____ **3**

    Vocational Rehabilitation _____ 3

    Social Security _____ 3

    Juvenile Justice _____ 5

    Behavioral Health _____ 6

    Workforce Investment _____ 7

    Themes Within and Across Systems _____ 8

    Conclusion _____ 9

    Table 1. Summary of Barriers, Recommendations, and Trends _____ 10

II.   **Introduction** _____ **12**

III. **Systems Overview** _____ **13**

    Vocational Rehabilitation _____ 13

    Social Security _____ 16

    Juvenile Justice _____ 20

    Behavioral Health _____ 22

    Workforce Investment _____ 23

IV. **Challenges and Barriers to Serving Youth with Disabilities** _____ **25**

    Vocational Rehabilitation _____ 25

    Social Security _____ 26

    Juvenile Justice _____ 27

    Behavioral Health _____ 28

    Workforce Investment _____ 30

V.   **Recommendations for Enhancing Systems' Capacity** _____ **32**

    Vocational Rehabilitation _____ 32

    Social Security _____ 35

    Juvenile Justice _____ 36

    Behavioral Health _____ 38

    Table 2. Elements of Recovery-Oriented Systems of Care _____ 39

    Workforce Investment _____ 41

VI. **Common Themes** _____ **44**

    Findings from Systematic Reviews _____ 44

    Trends Across Systems in the Literature _____ 44

    Conclusion _____ 49

VII. **Appendix A. Authorizing Legislation** _____ **50**

VIII. **Appendix B. Methodology** _____ **53**

    Table C-1. Research Databases in EBSCOhost _____ 53

IX. **References** _____ **55**

Tables

Table 1. Summary of Barriers, Recommendations, and Trends _____ 10

Table 2. Elements of Recovery-Oriented Systems of Care _____ 39

Table C-1. Research Databases in EBSCOhost _____ 53

I. Executive Summary

This study focused on five Federal systems[1] that play key and inter-related roles in preparing youth with disabilities as they transition into adulthood - vocational rehabilitation, social security, juvenile justice, behavioral health, and workforce investment. The study was limited to these five systems, rather than examining all of the systems that serve this population, due to financial constraints. This document summarizes each system's role, the extent of its use by the population, and central programs and authorizing legislation. In addition, challenges and recommendations for each system are identified, as are common themes and trends across systems. Table 1: Summary of Barriers, Recommendations, and Trends starting on page 10 summarizes these challenges and recommendations by system, as well as the common themes across systems.

Vocational Rehabilitation

The vocational rehabilitation (VR) system provides job skills training, counseling, college and university training, as well as support services for degree and non-degree programs to help youth with disabilities transition into self-sufficiency. These services are authorized by the Rehabilitation Act of 1973 (as amended). Altogether, in Fiscal Year (FY) 2011, around 180,000 transition age youth (TAY) had their VR records closed, which accounted for about 30 percent of VR closures (Koyanagi & Alfano, 2012).

The VR system covers a range of services for youth with disabilities, including mental health and substance abuse treatment, vocational training, higher education, medical services, independent living skills training, and employment-related services (Honeycutt, Thompkins, Bardos, & Stern, 2013). States vary in how they serve youth through the VR system. Eligibility for VR requires meeting the criteria set forth in the Rehabilitation Act of 1973 (Honeycutt et al., 2013). In 2007, the Study Group conducted an assessment of transition policies in state VR agencies for the Rehabilitation Services Administration. Among the 72 VR agencies that were surveyed for the study, 80 percent reported having individuals who coordinated transition services on a state level. The average caseload for VR counselors was 108. Within the 72 VR agencies, 63 percent of agencies had VR counselors with caseloads of TAY; 46 percent had counselors in local high schools, and 75 percent had counselors at American Job Centers (formerly known as One-Stop Career Centers) (The Study Group, 2007).

Challenges for serving TAY include low levels of participation in VR programs, wide variation across the country in VR programs, challenges to developing national standards for TAY in VR, a lack of research on VR services for TAY, a lack of effective collaboration with other agencies, ineffective state and local interagency agreements, and identification and referral barriers. To improve outcomes for TAY with disabilities, the vocational rehabilitation system is encouraged to provide opportunities for supported, integrated education and employment. Additionally, there is a need to build awareness of, and to promote use of, VR services for TAY. There has also been a call to develop VR program standards for serving TAY and building cultural competency. Families can also provide help TAY as they navigate the VR system. VR staff need additional opportunities for professional development and skill building to serve TAY. Finally, there is a need to improve partnerships between state and local education agencies (LEA) and VR agencies, change VR policy at Congressional level, and change VR's service structure at the Federal and state level.

Social Security

The Social Security Administration (SSA) provides support to individuals with disabilities through Supplemental Security Income (SSI) and Social Security Disability Insurance (SSDI). These programs were made a part of the Social Security Act of 1935, which was amended to create SSDI in 1954 and SSI in 1972. In 2011, 1.1 million youth (ages 13 to 25) received SSI benefits, and 213,000 youth (age 25 and under) received SSDI benefits; 12 percent of which were between the ages of 15 to 21 (Social Security Administration, 2012; Social Security Administration, 2013).

---

1 Due to funding limitations, this preliminary review of literature is focused on only five Federal systems and excludes other youth - and adult-service systems.

The SSI program provides income supplements to help cover basic needs for food, clothing, and shelter for those who are aged or have a disability, including being blind, and who have little or no income. Youth with disabilities under age 18 must include their parents' incomes and assets as part of the eligibility determination for SSI. Youth who are above age 18 do not have that requirement. The SSDI program provides income supplements for workers who have worked in jobs covered by Social Security and develop a medical condition that meets Social Security's definition of disability. According to the Social Security Administration's website, "disability" under Social Security is based on an individual's inability to work.

SSI beneficiaries may participate in the Plan to Achieve Self-Support (PASS) program with the goal of assisting an individual who wants to set aside money and/or things he or she owns to pay for items, services, or trainings needed to achieve a specific work goal. The PASS includes the steps and timeline that an individual will take to reach his/her employment goals. If the PASS is approved, the money that is spent towards the PASS plan does not count in terms of SSI eligibility (Social Security Administration, 2013b). The PASS program was included in the initial provisions of SSI in 1972 as a work incentive (Sheldon & Lopez-Soto, 2009).

The SSA's Ticket to Work program, which was authorized by the Ticket to Work and Work Incentives Improvement Act of 1999, is designed to help SSDI and SSI beneficiaries ages 18 through 64 receive rehabilitation and vocational services to get back to work or increase hours at work (Green, 2005; Social Security Administration, 2013). As of June 2006, around 10,000 Ticket to Work beneficiaries were working with an employment network (EN), and 130,000 were working with VR agencies (Green, 2005).

An EN is an entity that contracts with the Social Security Administration to either provide or coordinate the delivery of the necessary services in order to achieve the following goals: 1) Offer beneficiaries with disabilities expanded choices when seeking service and supports to enter, re-enter, and/or maintain employment; 2) Increase the financial independence and self-sufficiency of beneficiaries with disabilities; and 3) Reduce and, whenever possible, eliminate reliance on disability benefits. Under the Ticket to Work program, eligible SSDI and SSI beneficiaries who are receiving monthly cash benefits payments are entitled to participate by signing up with an approved service provider of their choice. This can be an EN or a state VR agency. The EN or state VR agency, if they accept the Ticket assignment, will coordinate and provide appropriate services to help the beneficiary find and maintain employment. These services may be training, career counseling, vocational rehabilitation, job placement, and ongoing support services necessary to achieve a work goal.[2] As of 2007, participation rates in the Ticket to Work program were only around 1.6 percent; however, 26 percent of disability beneficiaries reported that they saw themselves working for pay in the next five years (Thornton et al., 2007).

The Heroes Earning Assistance and Relief Act (HEART Act) of 1998 made national service more accessible to people with disabilities by directing SSA to exclude the AmeriCorps stipend and other benefits for determination of eligibility and calculation of monthly payment amounts for beneficiaries of SSI. Therefore AmeriCorps and AmeriCorps VISTA members can receive their stipend without losing benefits related to their disability. For SSI beneficiaries, this income exclusion also includes stipends received while participating in the AmeriCorps NCCC and AmeriCorps State and Local programs.

The Youth Transition Demonstration (YTD) was originally authorized by the 1980 Amendments to the Social Security Act and was initiated in 2003. The YTD is a random assignment research study designed to help youth with disabilities ages 14 to 25 to maximize their economic self-sufficiency as they transition from school to work. The YTD was designed to work with individuals who receive SSI or SSDI payments based on their own disability, or who are at risk of receiving SSI or SSDI benefits, and have an interest in pursuing a post-secondary education or an employment goal. The YTD funded six sites in five states - Colorado, Florida, Maryland, New York (Bronx and Erie), and West Virginia - to set up coordinated service delivery systems including individual work-based

---

2 Information retrieved from the Social Security Administration's website: http://ssa.gov/work/overview.html#ao=o.

experiences, youth empowerment, family supports, system linkages, social and health services, and benefits counseling (Green, 2005; Luecking & Wittenburg, 2009). Recognizing that a major barrier to employment for youth with disabilities is the fear of losing Social Security benefits, the YTD provides five waivers of program rules designed to allow participants to keep more of their earnings and encourage both savings and their continued education. These waivers allow:

1. Student Earned Income Exclusions regardless of age while in school;
2. Earned Income Exclusions of $65 plus $3 of every $4 earned;
3. Individual Development Accounts to save earnings plus funds from government and local providers;
4. Plans for Achieving Self-Support for career exploration and post-secondary education; and
5. Benefits to continue regardless of Continuing Disability Reviews and Age 18 Medical Redetermination results.[3]

All six random assignment sites completed their YTD participation and services as of March 2012, and the demonstration project and evaluation efforts are ongoing through 2014 (Mann & Wittenburg, 2012). This research is generating empirical evidence on the impacts of SSI waivers and enhanced coordination of services for youth with disabilities.

Challenges that the social security system faces in serving TAY with disabilities include overcoming disincentives to enter, re-enter, and maintain employment; accessing social security benefits; and preventing health insurance discontinuity. To address these challenges, the SSA needs to ensure policies are in place to encourage employment of disability beneficiaries, to promote coordination of services with VR agencies and special education systems, to increase the visibility of and participation in the Ticket to Work program, to support the advancement of research on program differences across states, and to reinstate the Social Security Student Benefit.

Juvenile Justice

The juvenile justice system must provide its transition-age youth with effective services not just to help them achieve a productive and independent adulthood, but also to help them adapt back into the community. In many cases, making a successful transition from incarceration back into the community and avoiding recidivism is a pre-determinant of successful transition to adulthood (Baltodano, Mathur & Rutherford, 2005). As much as 70 percent of the 110,000 youth incarcerated and 2.2 million youth arrested each year may have at least one diagnosable mental health disorder (Unruh, Waintrap, Canter & Smith, 2009). States report having anywhere from 9.1 percent to 77.5 percent of incarcerated youth eligible for and receiving special education services (Gagnon & Richards, 2008).

The Juvenile Justice and Delinquency Prevention Act (JJDPA) of 1974 provides conditions for how states must run juvenile justice facilities and programs. Two grant programs authorized under the JJDPA are the Juvenile Justice and Delinquency Prevention State Formula Grants and the Community Prevention Incentive Grants. Both are possible sources of funding for transition services, but those services are not the programs' main priority (Bazelon, 2008d). Similarly, the Safe Schools / Healthy Students program encourages local education agencies to collaborate with local mental health, law enforcement, and juvenile justice agencies to provide pro-social services for children, youth, and their families and could be a platform for transition services (Koyanagi & Alfano, 2012).

The educational needs of TAY with disabilities in the juvenile justice system are addressed by the Individuals with Disabilities Education Act (IDEA) and the No Child Left Behind (NCLB) Act. Under IDEA, Part B, youth under age 18 incarcerated in a juvenile facility are entitled to a free, appropriate, public education and, as with other youth served under IDEA, starting at age 16, Individualized Education Programs must include goals and services for transition (Leone & Weinberg, 2010; U.S. Department of Education, 2007). NCLB, Title I, Part D addresses the needs of youth who are imprisoned and authorizes transition-related activities such as counseling; psychological

---

and social work services; services for in-school advocates to act on behalf of individual children and youth who are neglected or delinquent; tutoring and mentoring; reentry orientation programs, including transition centers and reentry centers in high schools; instruction and training at alternative schools and learning centers; and parental involvement activities and parent counseling (U.S. Department of Education, 2006).

The juvenile justice system has internal challenges to adequately serving TAY with disabilities as well as having to address external issues that incarcerated youth often face. Internal challenges include a historic – though shifting – focus on punishment rather than rehabilitation for youth offenders (Lipsey, Howell, Kelly, Chapman & Carver, 2010). Incarcerated youth with disabilities have often previously received services from many other systems, including mental health, child welfare, and special education, making system coordination and service alignment challenging (Altschuler, Stangler, Berkley & Burton, 2009). The service providers in the juvenile justice system lack training in assisting youth with their transition needs (Leone & Weinberg, 2010). At the point of release, juvenile correctional facilities again have to interface with other systems and also new sections of its own system, such as parole (Altschuler, 2005; Hanger, 2008). The youth also face ineligibility for services because of their ex-offender status (Altschuler, 2005; Unruh, Povenmire-Kirk & Yamamoto, 2009). In addition, they may not have families to help them with the transition back to the community and into adulthood (Unruh, Povenmire-Kirk & Yamamoto, 2009).

Facing these challenges, the juvenile justice system needs to provide the youth in its care with many of the same transition services their non-justice involved peers need, but with some additions. In the context of transition for young offenders with disabilities, programming needs to start early after sentencing, encourage a sense of self-determination, engage youth in education and employment immediately after release, connect youth with positive peer role models and adult mentors, address gender differences in transition needs, and provide high-quality education and treatment services both in corrections and during the transition process (Baltodano, Mathur & Rutherford, 2010). The system can facilitate early and long-term engagement in employment by offering career preparation opportunities during confinement, and providing employment support after release (Hagner, Malloy, Mazzone & Cormier, 2008; Harris, 2006). The system may be able to better and more efficiently meet these goals by improving cross-system collaboration. Finally, the research and advocacy community is divided on the use of diversion and graduated sanctions to reduce the entry of youth into the juvenile justice system in the first place.

Behavioral Health

The mental health care system provides a crucial piece of the transition services puzzle. Beyond therapeutic/clinical interventions, the system can also support TAY by helping them stay engaged with their families, providing overall case management and service advocacy, helping them stay socially connected, and linking them to other needed services (Cavanaugh, 2009). The transition ages of 16 to 25 are a time when mental health service utilization declines, even though that may be when they are most needed because of the onset of substance use and mood disorders (Pottick et al., 2008). According to data from SAMHSA, 11.4 percent of TAY receive mental health services (SAMHSA, 2012).

States and localities provide mental health services with funding from the Federal government in the form of Mental Health Block Grants (MHBG) from the Center for Mental Health Services which have their roots in the Community Mental Health Centers Act in 1963 (National Institute of Mental Health, 2013). Transition-related services authorized under the MHBG include rehabilitation; employment; housing; education; substance abuse services; medical and dental care; services provided by local school systems under IDEA; and other support services (Bazelon Center for Mental Health Law, 2008b). Medicaid, authorized by Title XIX of the Social Security Act, also funds mental health services for youth and adults, though it is easier for youth to access such services with Medicaid (Bazelon Center for Mental Health Law, 2008a; Klees, Wolfe & Curtis, 2011). More recently, the Comprehensive Community Mental Health Services for Children and Their Families Program (also called the Children's Mental Health Initiative, or CMHI), authorized by the 1992 Alcohol, Drug Abuse and Mental Health Administration (ADAMHA) Reorganization Act, has been awarding funds to states and local communities to improve the coordination of services for children and youth up to age 21 with serious emotional disturbance.

Direct and indirect transition services are commonly provided under CMHI (Center for Mental Health Services, 2010).

There are significant challenges for TAY with disabilities receiving services from the mental health care system, largely related to funding. Because adolescents with disabilities may be covered by Medicaid, they face benefits redetermination at the age of majority: 18, 19, 20, or 21, depending on the state. Also, as they transition from the child mental health system to the adult mental health system, they have to navigate different illness definitions, different organizational cultures, changes in service providers, and poor coordination between the two systems (Bazelon, 2008; Davis, 2005; Helfinger, 2008; Pottick et al., 2008). As adults, doctor-patient confidentiality may pose a perceived barrier to their parents' and family members' participation in transition planning. On both sides of the child/adult system divide, transition services may be scarce or inappropriate for their needs and interests. Finally, while Medicaid waivers allow states to pursue innovative and promising approaches to serving TAY, even they have restrictions in use.

The mental health system can enhance its capacity to serve TAY with disabilities with focused attention on the needs of this population. Generally, providers should adopt a philosophy of recovery-oriented systems of care and utilize evidence-based practices. They could improve individual experiences by making sure that appealing, developmentally-appropriate services are available and accessible, and by providing support to help youth and families navigate systems that provide transition services (Davis, Geller & Hunt, 2006; Manteuffel, Stephens, Sondheimer & Fisher, 2008). On a state level, there is much that administrators could do to coordinate with other systems and bring attention to the needs of TAY with disabilities (Davis & Sondheimer, 2005; Davis, 2005; Woolsey & Katz-Leavy, 2008; GAO, 2008b). To fix the misalignment between child and adult mental health systems, states could designate responsibility for providing transition services, align eligibility between the systems, and/or extend Medicaid coverage (APA, n.d.; Hoffman, Heflinger, Athay & Davis, 2009).

Workforce Investment

The workforce investment system helps TAY through a variety of programs aimed to promote employment. The hallmark of the workforce investment system is American Job Centers, where individuals, including youth, can receive a variety of services related to employment, education, and job training. American Job Centers also provide access to vocational rehabilitation programs for people with disabilities. There is demand for these services; data from the National Longitudinal Transition Study-2 indicate that about 40 percent of youth with disabilities were not working, but 49 percent of that population was looking for paid employment (Newman et al., 2011). In 2008, 13.8 percent of youth served under workforce investment system reported disabilities (National Collaborative on Workforce & Disability for Youth, 2008).

The Workforce Investment Act of 1998 (WIA) mandated that American Job Centers provide coordinated and customer-focused services, including employment and training, adult education/literacy training, and vocational rehabilitation for adults, disadvantaged youth, and dislocated workers. Relevant to TAY with disabilities, WIA included a non-discrimination clause and provisions requiring states to help youth prepare for the workforce (Brown & Thakur, 2006; Center for Law and Social Policy, 2013; National Collaborative on Workforce & Disability for Youth, 2013). Title I provides for the formula-funded national Youth Service Program, as well as Job Corps, a primarily residentially-based education and training programs (National Collaborative on Workforce & Disability for Youth, 2013).

The workforce investment system provides a range of programs relevant to TAY with disabilities. The American Job Centers help youth 14 to 21 prepare for postsecondary education and employment, with services such as mentoring, training, continued services, incentives for achievement, and leadership development and community service opportunities (Koyanagi & Alfano, 2012). TAY with disabilities can also participate in U.S. Department of Labor apprenticeship programs, though its historical focus on the construction trade has been a challenge for serving youth with disabilities (Lynn & Mack, 2008). The Job Corps program provides education and training for economically disadvantaged youth age 16 to 24 (Koball, 2011); the program employs regional disability coordinators to serve participants with disabilities (Lynn & Mack, 2008). Finally, the YouthBuild program serves out-of-school youth age 16 to 24, including those with disabilities, with on-the-job training and internship opportunities as well as other employment and educational services (Koyanagi & Alfano, 2012). The workforce investment system could better reach TAY with disabilities by offering longer lasting, multifaceted programming (Bloom, Thompson, & Ivry, 2010). There may also be a disincentive for agencies to serve the hardest to serve who need long term support due to performance measurement requirements (GAO, 2010; Larson, 2009). Similar to other systems, staff in the workforce investment system could benefit from specific training on serving TAY with disabilities and youth as they often need assistance in navigating and coordinating system services. The workforce system is also criticized for over-reliance on segregated work opportunities for people with disabilities and not utilizing universal design principles (APHSA, 2012; Carter et al., 2010).

American Job Centers and other workforce investment programs have the mission and capacity to serve more TAY with disabilities and serve them better. The National Center on Workforce and Disability encourages American Job Centers to coordinate with local schools and transition teams, communicate with parent groups, explore interagency agreements, and become involved in the local workforce investment board or Youth Councils in order to better reach this population (National Center on Workforce & Disability, n.d.). In addition, they could offer supported education and employment opportunities. Important service areas for TAY achieving employment are community linkages, work supports, family involvement, and student involvement (Carter & Lunsford, 2005). The system could also make more of an effort to engage a diversity of youth with disabilities.

Themes Within and Across Systems

There are several common trends in the issues and recommendations for systems serving TAY with disabilities. Some, such as aligning eligibility and access and helping youth navigate services, are client-facing that will impact how youth and their families experience transition services. Others, like collaboration and coordination, are more administrative and will require action at the Federal, state, and agency levels.

Client eligibility and access to services are shaped by statutory, administrative, and practical factors. A major criticism of programming for TAY is that there is inconsistency in the age limits of programs (GAO, 2008b; Koyanagi & Alfano, 2012). Many suggest increasing youth services through age 24 or 25 to cover the transition period and provide "continuity of care," or cross-training adult service providers to reach transitioning youth (Altschuler, 2005; Bridgeland & Mason-Elder, 2012; Davis, n.d.; Davis & Sondheimer, 2005; Hoffman, Heflinger, Athay & Davis, 2009; Koyanagi & Alfano, 2012; Manteuffel, Stephens, Sondheimer & Fisher, 2008; Stewart, et al., 2010).

Increasing participation in programs is also a consideration for all systems. Increasing participation goes beyond strategies to changing eligibility rules; it also requires enhancing providers' service capacity, delivering age-appropriateness programs, accessibility, and ensuring services are appealing to TAY (Davis, Geller, & Hunt, 2006).

Youth and their families need supports to help them navigate services available, both within each system and across the systems (Heflinger & Hoffman, 2008; Podmostko, 2007; Stewart et al., 2010). In a qualitative study of youth involved in the Social Security Administration's Youth Transition Demonstration, one-on-one relationships with counselors were vital to maintaining youth's drive to find work and to navigate the system (O'Day, 2012).

On a related note, agencies and systems could improve their services and outcomes by increasing collaboration and coordination. Researchers from the Bazelon Center for Mental Health Law point out that there is no "overarching framework for systems and service integration" (Koyanagi & Alfano, 2012). Differing eligibility rules, as mentioned above, are one reason, but other factors include differing agency cultures, lack of interagency agreements, differing perspectives on the correct and appropriate ways to treat youth population (especially in the context of juvenile justice), and a lack of funding for collaboration and coordination. Suggestions for improving coordination, therefore, include integrated eligibility reviews, instituting formal referral processes, and continuing the work of Federal interagency working groups (GAO, 2008b; Sturgis, 2013). Researchers who have analyzed policies around vulnerable youth have also suggested developing a single national policy focused on youth in transition (Fernandes, 2012; Moreno, Honeycutt, McLeod, & Gill, 2013). State agencies could thus be influenced to coordinate services and planning, and engage in continuous quality improvement of their transition efforts (Gonsoulin, Darwin & Read, 2012).

To translate such changes in Federal and state policy into practice, service providers in the various systems serving TAY with disabilities would benefit from further specific training and professional development (Grigal et al., 2011; Hoffman, Heflinger, Athay & Davis, 2009; Leone & Weinberg, 2010; Plotner, Trach, & Strauser, 2012; Osgood, et al., 2011; Stewart et al., 2010; The Study Group, 2007; Woolsey & Katz-Leavy, 2008). Broadly, the American Psychological Association recommends developing a professionally trained mental and behavioral health workforce that can meet the needs of children, TAY, and adults with severe mental illness (APA, n.d.). A specific type of training that might benefit transition service providers is in delivering culturally-appropriate services (Balcazar et al., 2013). Existing transition practices may not fit the needs, values, and family circumstances of culturally and linguistically diverse (CLD) youth (Povenmire-Kirk, Lindstrom, & Bullis, 2010). These youth and their families should be engaged with more person-centered planning (Trainor, 2010).

Finally, additional research is needed on what services achieve the intended outcomes and how agencies have been able to coordinate services to maximize impact. Pilot projects and demonstration projects are key to advancing the state of knowledge in the field, teasing apart best practices, and exploring model replication (Stewart et al., 2010; Woolsey & Katz-Leavy, 2008). Additional research providing data on this population has the ability to be utilized as a policy tool to drive attention to this population and the performance of the publicly funded service systems (Heflinger & Hoffman, 2008).

Conclusion

These five Federal systems - Vocational Rehabilitation, Social Security, Juvenile Justice, Behavioral Health, and Workforce Investment – each have opportunities to influence the transition of youth with disabilities who receive their services. Table 1: Summary of Barriers, Recommendations, and Trends on page 16 summarizes each system's challenges and recommendations to serving these youth effectively, as well as the common themes across systems, found in the literature.

Table 1. Summary of Barriers, Recommendations, and Trends

	Challenges and Barriers	Recommendations
Vocational Rehabilitation	• Low Levels of Participation in VR Programs • Wide Variation Across the Country in VR Programs • Developing National Standards for TAY in VR • Lack of Research on VR Services for TAY • Lack of Effective Collaboration with Other Agencies • Ineffective State and Local Interagency Agreements • Identification and Referral Barriers	• Enhance Supported, Integrated Education and Employment • Build Awareness of, and Promote Use of, VR Services • Integrate VR and Medicaid • Develop VR Program Standards for TAY • Build Cultural Competency • Involve Family in Career Planning • Create Additional Professional Development Opportunities for VR Staff • Enhance VR Counselor Skills • Improve State LEA and VR Partnerships • Change VR Policy at Congressional Level • Change Service Structure at Federal and State Level
Social Security	• Disincentives to Enter, Re-enter, and Maintain Employment • Accessing Social Security Benefits • Health Insurance Discontinuity	• Revise Policy to Encourage Employment • Coordinate Services with VR agencies and special education systems • Increase Visibility of and Participation in the TTW program • Increase Research on Program Differences across States • Reinstate Social Security Student Benefit
Juvenile Justice	• Focus on Punishment Rather than Rehabilitation • Fragmentation of Services • Post Release Barriers • Lack Support of Family and Home Life • Lack of Training for Service Providers Within the Juvenile Justice System	• Offer High Quality Transition Programming As Soon As Youth Receive Sentencing • Encourage Self-Determination • Engage Youth in Education, Treatment, Career Preparation, and Employment Services Both in Corrections and During Transition After Release • Connect Youth with Positive Peer Role Models and Adult Mentors • Address Gender Differences in Transition Needs • Improve Cross-System Collaboration • Consider the Use of Diversion and Graduated Sanctions to Prevent Youth from Entering the Juvenile Justice System

	Challenges and Barriers	Recommendations
Behavioral Health	• Insurance Benefits Redetermination and Service Discontinuity • Medicaid Waiver Restrictions • Navigate Different Illness Definitions, Different Organizational Cultures, Changes in Service Providers, between Child and Adult Systems • Scarcity of Appropriate Services • Confidentiality Barriers to Family Participation	• Adopt Recovery-Oriented Systems Of Care • Provide Appealing, Developmentally-Appropriate Services • Assert State Leadership for Interagency Coordination • Establish System Responsibility for Providing Services • Align Eligibility in the Youth and Adult Service Systems • Improve Availability of Services • Provide Support for Navigating System Transition • Promote the Use of Evidence-Based Approaches • Train Service Providers to Specialize in Transition • Increase State and Federal Attention to the Needs of TAY
Workforce Investment	• Difficulty with System Change and Lack of Multifaceted, Intense Programming • Insufficient Staff Training and Funding • Eligibility and Accessibility • Difficulty with Program Compliance • Operating with Budget Cuts	• Promote Inclusive Employment and Access to Workforce Investment Services • Better Engage American Job Centers • Increase Supported Education and Employment to Build Skills • Coordinate Services and Improve Navigability • Engage Diverse (Low-Income, Minority, ESL) Youth • Enhance Summer Employment • Revisit Performance Measures and Build Data Systems

Trends Across Systems	• Adopt Student Focused Planning
	• Allow Flexibility in Providing Tailored Supports
	• Fund Additional Research and Empirically-Validated Studies
	• Improve Eligibility and Access
	  ▪ Align Age Limits and Increase the Upper Bounds of Service Eligibility
	  ▪ Align Child and Adult Definitions of Illness
	  ▪ Simplify Benefit Programs and Work Incentives
	  ▪ Increase Participation in Transition Programs
	  ▪ Develop Comprehensive, Coordinated, Age-Appropriate, Youth-Driven Services
	• Improve Collaboration and Coordination
	  ▪ Align Child and Adult Service Systems
	  ▪ Integrate Service Systems Using Formal Processes
	  ▪ Hold Service Systems Accountable
	  ▪ Develop Appropriate Data Systems
	  ▪ Encourage Coordination at the Federal Level
	  ▪ Promote a Single National Collaborative Policy
	  ▪ Promote Coordinated, Focused Planning and Accountability
	• Ensure Staff Training and Professional Development for Service Providers
	• Tailor Transition Services for Culturally and Linguistically Diverse (CLD) Youth
	• Help Youth Navigate Services	

II. Introduction

In a response to the GAO 2012 report, entitled *Students with Disabilities: Better Federal Coordination Could Lessen Challenges in the Transition from High School*, which stated that limited coordination among youth programs hinders a successful transition for students with disabilities, the Office of Disability Employment Policy (ODEP) requested a literature review limited, due to financial constraints, to five youth service delivery systems.

This study provides an overview of relevant literature related to these five Federal systems[4] that support youth with disabilities as they transition into adulthood: vocational rehabilitation, social security, juvenile justice, behavioral health, and the workforce investment system. The literature search focused on seven key questions of interest to ODEP:

- What role does each system play in youth transition?
- To what extent (e.g., number of youth served, number of youth estimated to be eligible for services, etc.), are youth with disabilities being served by each of these systems?
- What legislation authorizes the program(s)?
- What are the central programs and services for youth with disabilities provided by each system?
- According to the literature, what are the challenges and barriers to serving youth with disabilities in the systems?
- According to the literature, what are the recommendations (both state and Federal) for enhancing systems' capacity to serve youth with disabilities?
- According to the literature, what are common themes or trends around transition both within and across systems?

This literature review starts by providing an introduction to the five systems of interest, including their role in youth transition, the extent to which youth with disabilities are served, and their central programs offering transition-related services. The next two sections deal with challenges and recommendations, respectively, and are organized by system. The final section addresses common themes recognized among the systems.

Appendix A provides authorizing legislation for the major programs, by system. Appendix B then describes the research methods used in conducting this literature review. In short, we used a phased progression of collecting data, which included examining resources provided by ODEP, conducting independent searches, and engaging subject matter experts. Appendix B also lists databases and keywords used in the searches. This approach allowed us to answer all the research questions posed above and present a thorough examination of existing research on the topic of transition services for youth with disabilities by these five systems.

Transition age youth (TAY) with disabilities represent an at-risk population for disconnection. It is estimated that 6.7 million 16 to 24 year olds are disconnected, many of which have mental and physical health conditions and are involved in the criminal justice system (Belfield, Levin, & Rosen, 2012). Some data show that around 16.8 percent of disconnected youth have a severe disability and are receiving Supplemental Security Income (SSI) or Medicaid (322,000), 14.7 percent have a severe disability and are not receiving Medicare/SSI (281,000), and 2.2 percent have a non-severe disability (42,000) (Fernandes & Gabe, 2009). Findings from the 2010 American Community Survey indicated that youth with disabilities are enrolled in school or employed at much lower rates than youth without disabilities (Smith, Grigal, & Sulewsi, 2012).

Recent large-scale surveys revealed the number of youth with work limitations. The Survey of Income Program Participation revealed that 3 percent of youth ages 18 to 24 had work limitations, but when using a broader definition of disabilities, related to their effects on instrumental activities of daily living, the percentage increased to 9 percent. The National Health Interview Survey revealed that eight percent of youth had limitations due to

---

4 Due to funding limitations, this preliminary review of literature is focused on only five Federal systems and excludes other youth - and adult-service systems.

chronic conditions. In 2005, 6 million youth ages 6 to 21 participated in special education services under the Individuals with Disabilities Education Act (Honeycutt & Wittenburg, 2012). Thus, this is an important population to engage in services to promote education and employment for ultimate long-term self-sufficiency.

III. Systems Overview

This section describes each system in detail in relation to how the system serves TAY with disabilities. An overview is provided of how the system serves TAY, the programs that serve TAY within each system, and the literature, where available, that describes the number of TAY served and their outcomes. Information about each system's authorizing legislation is provided in Appendix A.

Vocational Rehabilitation

The vocational rehabilitation (VR) system provides important support for eligible TAY with disabilities. VR programs help provide students with disabilities job skill training, assessment, job placement, job coaching, counseling, college and university training, as well as support and financial support services for degree and non-degree programs to help them transition into self-sufficiency. The Rehabilitation Act of 1973, as amended, authorizes the formula grant programs of vocational rehabilitation, supported employment, independent living, and client assistance. It also authorizes training and service discretionary grants administered by the Rehabilitation Services Administration within the U.S. Department of Education (U.S. Department of Education, 2013). The Rehabilitation Act was reauthorized under the WIA of 1998 (National Council on Disability, 2008). Both the Rehabilitation Act and the Individuals with Disabilities Education Act allow states to "establish parameters to guide the participation of vocational rehabilitation counselors in the Individualized Education Program (IEP) transition planning process" (National Council on Disability, 2008). The IEP is the "cornerstone of the transition process" which includes the expected employment outcome for the individual and steps toward helping the individual meet that goal. The IEP is put together by a team of individuals, which frequently include the VR counselor, secondary school personnel, and the student themselves (National Council on Disability, 2008).

Priority for vocational rehabilitation is given to participants with the most severe disabilities, and those eligible for SSI are presumed eligible. VR agencies provide services, which include comprehensive assessment, counseling, vocational training, transportation, transitional services, and supported employment services (Koyanagi & Alfano, 2012). The Rehabilitation Act defines transition as a "a coordinated set of activities for a student, designed within an outcome oriented process, that promotes movement from school to post school activities, including postsecondary education, vocational training, integrated employment (including supported employment), continuing and adult education, adult services, independent living, or community participation" (The Study Group, 2007).

Vocational Rehabilitation Services Program. The VR services program provides individualized services to meet the specific needs of the individual with disabilities. This program provides grants to states to support a wide range of services designed to help individuals with disabilities prepare for, and engage in, gainful employment consistent with their strengths, resources, priorities, concerns, abilities, capabilities, interests, and informed choice. According to the U.S. Department of Education, eligible individuals are those who have a physical or mental impairment that results in a substantial impediment to employment, who can benefit from VR services for employment, and who require VR services. Priority must be given to serving individuals with the most significant disabilities if a state is unable to serve all eligible individuals. Funds are distributed to states and territories based on a formula that takes into account population and per capita income to cover the cost of direct services and program administration. Grant funds are administered under an approved state plan by VR agencies designated by each state. The state-matching requirement is 21.3 percent; however, the state share is 50 percent for the cost of construction of a facility for community rehabilitation program purposes.[5]

---

5 Information retrieved from U.S. Department of Education's website: http://www2.ed.gov/programs/rsasupemp/index.html.

Supported Employment Services program. This program provides grants to assist states in developing and implementing collaborative programs with appropriate entities to provide programs of supported employment services for individuals with the most significant disabilities who require supported employment services to achieve employment outcomes. Grant funds are administered under a state plan supplement to the Title I of the Rehabilitation Act state plan for VR services designated by each state. Supported employment grant funds are used to supplement funds provided under the state VR grants program for the costs of providing supported employment services. According to the U.S. Department of Education, program funds may be used to supplement assessments under the Title I program and supplement other VR services necessary to help individuals with the most significant disabilities find work in the integrated labor market. Funds cannot be used to provide the extended services necessary to maintain individuals in employment after the end of supported employment services, which usually do not exceed 18 months.

Independent Living Services program. According to the U.S. Department of Education, this program offers formula grants to states for one or more of the following purposes:
- To provide resources to statewide independent living councils (SILCs);
- To provide independent living (IL) services to individuals with significant disabilities;
- To demonstrate ways to expand and improve IL services;
- To support the operation of centers for IL that comply with the standards and assurances of Section 725 of the Rehabilitation Act;
- To support activities to increase the capabilities of public or nonprofit agencies and organizations and other entities in developing comprehensive approaches or systems for providing IL services;
- To conduct studies and analyses and gather information, approaches, strategies, findings, conclusions, and recommendations for Federal, state, and local policymakers to enhance IL services for individuals with significant disabilities;
- To provide training on the IL philosophy; and
- To provide outreach to populations that are unserved or underserved by programs under Title VII of the Rehabilitation Act, including minority groups and urban and rural populations.[6]

Service Use and Data on TAY with Disabilities. In Fiscal Year (FY) 2011, around 180,000 TAY had their VR records closed, which was around 30 percent of the VR closures (Koyanagi & Alfano, 2012). Research has shown that less than eight percent of students with disabilities exit school with a job, enroll in post-secondary education, attend community recreation or are in independent living (Condon & Callahan, 2008). Using the Case Service Report RSA-911 closure data, from 2004 to 2006, 8 percent of youth with disabilities (16 to 24) applied for vocational rehabilitation, and 56 percent who applied received services, and 2.3 percent who received services were employed when services ended. TAY, ages 16 to 24, account for one-third of the vocational rehabilitation service population. From 2004 to 2006, 40.7 percent of VR applicants were female, 74.0 percent were white, and 61.6 percent had less than a high school education. Fifty-two percent had an intellectual disability, 25.0 percent had psychiatric disability, 11.7 percent physical disability, and 5.8 percent sensory disability. Additionally, most applicants (45.1 percent) were referred from educational institutions (elementary and secondary) (Honeycutt, Thompkins, Bardos, & Stern, 2013). [7]

In 2008, the National Council on Disability issued a report on outcomes for transition aged youth. Overall, they found that VR has been increasingly serving TAY; however, VR is serving a small percentage of youth who may be eligible for VR services (NCD, 2008). In a study of RSA-911 data on learning disabilities, the data show that young adults with learning disabilities make up 5 percent (around 30,000) of the population that VR is serving; however, it is estimated that 2.8 million students with learning disabilities received special education services in 2006 to 2007 (Gonzalez, Rosenthal, & Kim, 2011).

---

6 Information retrieved from the U.S. Department of Education's website: http://www2.ed.gov/programs/rsailstate/index.html.

7 Newer data on VR is available here: www.rsa.ed.gov but our scope did not include primary data collection.

The 1992 Amendments to the Rehabilitation Act mandated an evaluation of VR. The evaluation included a random sample of 40 VR offices, which included 8,500 applicants. Results were weighted to provide an overall estimate for the 956 VR offices. The VR programs deliver services across both rural and urban locations. In particular, the findings show that four percent of the population is limited by a disability in terms of the type of work they can complete, and five percent are prevented from working at all. The majority of beneficiaries are 86 percent white and 10 percent are African-American. One-third of participants have a high school education, 22 percent have less than a high school education, and 18 percent have a bachelor's degree. For the most part, vocational rehabilitation managers estimate that 31 percent of employment that participants achieve is in service occupations (Hayward & Schmidt-Davis, 2005).

States vary in how they serve youth through the vocational rehabilitation system. Eligibility for vocational rehabilitation requires meeting criteria set forth in the Rehabilitation Act of 1973 (Honeycutt, Thompkins, Bardos, & Stern, 2013). Using RSA-911 data, Honeycutt and colleagues found considerable state-level variation of VR services for TAY. The percentage of TAY applying for VR ranged from 4 to 14 percent, those receiving services ranged from 31 to 82 percent, and 40 to 70 percent had cases closed due to employment from 2004 to 2006. Across the country, the percentage of the VR applicants that received federal disability benefits (SSI or SSDI) at application ranged from 10 to 44 percent (Honeycutt et al., 2013).

Additionally, across the country, the types of services that VR can refer participants to vary based on availability. VR managers reporting services in their areas are at the following percentages:
- 60 percent mental health and substance abuse treatment
- 56 percent vocational training
- 51 percent higher education
- 47 percent medical services
- 15 percent independent living skills training
- 81 percent Employment Security Commission
- 66 percent Employment-related services under the Job Training Partnership Act/Workforce Investment Act (JTPA/WIA)
- 33 percent Projects with industry

Specific services associated with improved outcomes include having a productive and helpful relationship between client and counselor (as reported by the client), enrollment in postsecondary education, and receipt of health benefits (Hayward & Schmidt-Davis, 2005). Preliminary findings from a qualitative study of VR agencies revealed that all agencies interviewed had collaborations with other agencies and targeted programs for youth, but there was insufficient capacity to serve all who are eligible (some programs had as small as ten participants). Successful agencies targeted out of school youth, had a large population of youth who applied before age 18, and provided a variety of services (Honeycutt, 2013).

In 2007, the Study Group conducted an assessment of transition policies in State VR agencies for the Rehabilitation Services Administration. Among the studied 72 VR agencies surveyed, 80 percent reported having individuals who coordinate transition on a state level. The average caseload for VR counselors was 108. Sixty-three percent of agencies had counselors with caseloads of TAY, 46 percent had counselors in local high schools, and 75 percent had counselors at American Job Centers, formerly known as One-Stop Career Centers. They identified the most frequently used and effective policies and practices across a variety of domains (The Study Group, 2007). For state and local interagency agreements, the most effective policies and practices included agreements established with individual school districts in the state, VR agencies working with local educational agencies to "identify barriers within each organization that may impede the local delivery of transition services," and local agreements that specifically identify the role that each agency will play (The Study Group, 2007). In terms of identification, referral, and application, the state VR staff use school records for eligibility determinations and the VR agencies provide materials to the school staff to provide referrals to VR. VR and education agencies work together to develop how to best outreach to TAY (The Study Group, 2007). The policies and practices perceived to be the most effective was VR participating in transition planning meetings for TAY prior to high school completion. Other policies and practices perceived as effective include VR staff providing counseling while students are still in school, as well as follow-up to students once they finish high school to help them navigate postsecondary education and employment. The VR staff can also work with the schools to help give students work-based training experiences. Successful partnerships between VR agencies and schools were perceived as most effective where both entities shared the cost of transition programming, and where the state could track funding on TAY (The Study Group, 2007).

Balcazar, Oberoi, and Keel (2013) reviewed VR data from a Midwest state to look at transition outcomes for youth with disabilities, which included 26,292 transition cases. Findings show that youth with a sensory disability were more likely to have employment or postsecondary enrollment. Additionally, youth had a higher change of achieving competitive employment if they had more money spent on their case, and those who had on the job support and guidance were more likely to achieve employment, rather than postsecondary education (Balcazar, Oberoi, & Keel, 2013).

Social Security

The Social Security Administration (SSA) provides support to individuals with disabilities through Supplemental Security Income (SSI) and Social Security Disability Insurance (SSDI). SSI provides benefits to children and adults with disabilities with limited income. SSDI provides benefits to individuals with disabilities who are restricted in their ability to work, but also provides work incentives to help beneficiaries access employment opportunities, in particular, through their Plan for Achieving Self-Support (PASS program). Individuals eligible for Social Security benefits are also eligible for VR services, as outlined above, and are referred to VR programs through Social Security work incentive programs like Ticket to Work and the school system they are receiving special education services from.

Social Security was established in 1935 to provide retirement benefits for older adults (Guzman, Pirog, & Seefeldt, 2013). Amendments to the law added Social Security Disability Insurance (1954 as Title II) and Supplemental Security Income (1972 as Title XVI). The programs provide income support and health benefits for youth (and adults) with disabilities (National Collaborative on Workforce & Disability for Youth, 2013). The Social Security Act defines disability strictly and includes complex eligibility requirements (Green, Eigen, Lefko, & Ebling, 2005). Recently, the SSA made a policy change to allow youth with disabilities transitioning out of foster care to apply for SSI benefits 90 days prior to their eighteenth birthday, as opposed to 30 days. This change was designed to reduce the potential for a gap in benefits for these youth. Preliminary findings from an SSA study concluded that the policy change may have led to earlier SSI applications. However, the preliminary findings show that the policy change did not affect outcomes of SSI applications for youth transitioning out of foster care (King & Rukh-Kamaa, 2013). This could be due to the lack of knowledge about this rule change by social service providers.

The SSA has also implemented demonstration programs for youth with disabilities to promote transition into adulthood, in particular, the Youth Transition Demonstration and most recently the Promoting Readiness of Minors in Supplemental Security Income (PROMISE) initiative. Again, Ticket to Work is a program for youth age 18 and older. The SSA defines transition from school to economic self-sufficiency by way of postsecondary education or employment for youth who receive or are at risk of receiving SSI or SSDI benefits based on their own disability (Social Security Administration, 2012). According to the Marriott Foundation's Bridges From School to Work Program, although postsecondary employment outcomes for transition-age youth with disabilities have improved over the past decade, minority youth with disabilities continue to lag behind their peers in achieving a job. This study of predominantly minority youth participating in the Marriott Foundation's Bridges From School to Work Program from 2000 to 2005 analyzed data for 4,571 urban youth to determine what factors are associated with securing employment, and the nature of the jobs that are secured. Findings indicated that 68 percent of the youth in the program secured a job, a rate considerably higher than the national average. Results of the study also indicate that gender, previous vocational experience, and receipt of Social Security benefits were among the significant factors predicting employment (Fabian, 2007).

SSI. Supplemental Security Income provides income supplements to adults and children with severe disabilities (Green et al., 2005). Children are eligible for SSI according to their parents' income and assets. When children reach 18, eligibility is no longer determined by their parents' income and assets, but their own. As of August 2013, around 8.3 million individuals received SSI, 1.3 million of which were under the age of 18 (Social Security Administration, 2013a).

In order to qualify for SSI, applicants 18 or older must show that they are unable to engage in work due to a "medically determinable impairment that is expected to last at least 12 months or result in death" and must also qualify based on their income and assets (Ben-Shalom, Stapleton, Phelps, & Bardos, 2012). In an evaluation of SSI disability beneficiaries, younger beneficiaries were more likely to access employment than older counterparts (Ben-Shalom, Stapleton, Phelps, & Bardos, 2012).

SSDI. Social Security Disability Insurance provides income assistance for workers who have become disabled. If a worker's earnings exceed a certain level, she is no longer eligible for SSDI, which may create a real or perceived work disincentive (Guzman, Pirog, & Seefeldt, 2013). SSDI provides assistance to children who have been disabled since before age 22 (Green et al., 2005). Unlike SSI, SSDI is not means tested but "requires the individual to have worked and contributed to the Disability Insurance (DI) Trust Fund via payroll taxes for a sufficient period to attain "disability-insured status" (Ben-Shalom, Stapleton, Phelps, & Bardos, 2012).

In December 2011, 9.8 million individuals received SSDI, 87.5 percent of which were disabled workers (Social Security Administration, 2011). In 2011, 1.1 million youth (ages 13 to 25) received SSI benefits, and 213,000 youth (age 25 and under) received SSDI, 12 percent of which were between the ages of 15 to 21 (Social Security Administration, 2012). Data show that between 1996 and 2007, the composition of Social Security disability awardees changed for individuals under the age of 40. Specifically, in 2007 as opposed to 1996, more SSDI benefits were given to disabled adult children than disabled workers, those who had received SSI in the past and individuals who had psychiatric disorders than other types of disabilities (Ben-Shalom & Stapleton, 2013).

Using longitudinal data, Liu and Stapleton (2011) reviewed data for individuals who began to receive SSI from 1996 to 2006. For the cohort beginning in 1996, 46.1 percent were still receiving the benefit in 2006, and 40 percent did not use SSDI work incentives. Of the 53.9 percent that had left the rolls, most had left for reasons other than work. Twenty-one percent of the 1996 cohort returned to work by 2006, and of those returning to work, they were more likely to find work and use work incentives during their first 5 years of receiving the benefit. Younger beneficiaries, ages 18 to 39, were much more likely to leave the rolls and return to work than older beneficiaries (Liu & Stapleton, 2011).

Medicaid. Medicaid is authorized by Title XIX of the Social Security Act and eligibility is linked in the majority of states to SSI receipt. Medicaid is operated as a partnership between the Center for Medicare and Medicaid Services and the states which administer the program, and thus may set eligibility and service standards above Federal minimums. Individuals are considered for Medicaid eligibility purposes until age 19, 20, or 21, depending on the state (Bazelon Center for Mental Health Law, 2008a). Under Medicaid's Early and Periodic Screening, Diagnostic, and Treatment (EPSDT) requirement, states are required to provide comprehensive health and developmental assessments, and vision, dental and hearing services to children and youth, whereas states can be more restrictive in services they provide to adults. Furthermore, the definition of "medically necessary" services is broader for children than for adults, to the degree that it includes services that will "improve the chances of leading fuller and more independent lives" (Williams & Tolbert, 2007), opening the door for coverage of transition services.

Additionally, Medicaid's 1915(i) state waiver program allows states to provide a variety of services relevant to TAY with disabilities, including intensive care coordination, respite, parent and youth support partners, housing counseling, behavioral counseling, housing and vehicle modifications, and assistive technology (Mann & Hyde, 2013; Poisal & Cooper, n.d.). One additional service that may be particularly appropriate for TAY is "Flex Funds" (allowable under 1915(i) and select other waivers) which can be used for non-recurring, set-up expenses such as furniture (Mann & Hyde, 2013).

The Affordable Care Act (ACA) of 2010 allows states to expand their Medicaid programs to cover more qualifying children. In addition, the ACA made changes to Medicaid's 1915(i) program in the areas of expanding eligibility and eligibility protections, giving states flexibility to create new Medicaid categories to reach new populations, offering new services and target services to particular groups, and reducing states' ability to limit program availability (FamiliesUSA, n.d.; Klees, Wolfe & Curtis, 2011).

Plan for Achieving Self-Support (PASS). The PASS is a program through the SSA to help beneficiaries set aside money and/or things he or she owns to pay for items, services, or trainings needed to move towards employment. The PASS includes the steps and timeline that an individual will take to reach his/her employment goals. If the PASS is approved, the money that is spent towards the PASS plan does not count in terms of SSI eligibility (Social Security Administration, 2013b). The PASS program was included in the initial provisions of SSI in 1972 as a work incentive (Sheldon & Lopez-Soto, 2009).

Student Earned Income Exclusion. The SSA provides a provision for individuals, ages under the age of 22, who are receiving SSI and attending school to exclude their earnings from income. Students must be attending a college or university at least eight hours a week, grades 7-12 for 12 hours a week, an employment training course for at least 12 hours a week, or home schooled for 12 hours per week. In January 2013, individuals could exclude $1,730 monthly, up to a maximum of $6,960 per year (Social Security Administration, 2013d).

Ticket to Work. The Ticket to Work and Work Incentives Improvement Act of 1999 - Public Law 106-170 authorized the Ticket to Work Program. An individual, ages 18 through 62, must be receiving SSDI or Supplemental Security Income (SSI), and must have a disability for which medical improvement is not expected or possible; the individual must live in a state where Tickets are available (National Collaborative on Workforce & Disability for Youth, 2013). The law was built on the idea that individuals with disabilities have opportunities to find work, and addressed criticism that SSDI and SSI beneficiaries have disincentives to find work – in 1999, less than .05 percent of beneficiaries returned to work (Green et al., 2005).

The SSA's Ticket to Work program is designed to help beneficiaries receive rehabilitation and vocational services to get back to work or increase hours at work (Green et al., 2005; Social Security Administration, 2013c). Specifically, beneficiaries receive a "ticket" to voluntarily access an employment network or vocational rehabilitation. In 2005, the SSA mailed around 75,000 tickets per month. As of June 2006, approximately 10,000 beneficiaries were working with an employment network (EN), and 130,000 were working with VR agencies (Green et al., 2005). If beneficiaries receive SSI because of a disability, they are categorically eligible to receive services from vocational rehabilitation programs (Social Security Administration, 2013c). Vocational rehabilitation programs work with individuals who need more intensive services, such as training and education. Employment Networks are organizations that provide vocational rehabilitation, employment and other support services. As a part of Ticket to Work, Social Security may postpone Continuing Disability Reviews if the participant is making progress towards achieving employment (Social Security Administration, 2013c).

According to a 2007 Ticket to Work evaluation, participation rates were low in 2007 at around 1.6 percent; however, 26 percent of disability beneficiaries reported that they saw themselves working for pay in the next five years. The program did increase access to employment services. The evaluation also revealed that participants using tickets for employment networks received fewer services that those who used state vocational rehabilitation agencies and were less satisfied with services (Thornton et al., 2007). Additionally, findings from a 2010 Ticket to Work evaluation revealed that SSI and SSDI awardees have challenges to work, but many had high employment expectations, and those who worked had strong ties in their jobs. Younger beneficiaries (age 18 to 40) were the most likely age group to seek employment (Livermore & Stapleton, 2010).

In an updated evaluation of the Ticket to Work Program, it was found that increased Ticket mailings increased enrollment in services, and in particular, service enrollment was increased if the Ticket was received early in the rollout period, as opposed to later in the rollout. However, there were no impacts on benefits suspended or terminated for work or nonpayment status following suspension or termination for work (Stapleton, Mamun, & Page, 2013).

Reintegration of Ex-Offenders. SSA's Reintegration of Ex-Offenders program provides funding for services for youth offenders, including pre-release, mentoring, housing, case management, and employment services. One of the more recently funded initiatives is the Serving Juvenile Offenders in High-Poverty, High Crime Communities grant program, which provides for workforce development, education and training, case management, mentoring, and restorative justice. As of 2012, none of the Reintegration of Ex-Offenders programs have specifically targeted youth with disabilities (Fernandes-Alcantara, 2012).

Youth Transition Demonstration. The Youth in Transition Demonstration was authorized by sections 234 and 1110 of the Social Security Act of 1935, which was amended in 1980 by Public Law 96-265. The amendments authorized demonstration projects to help beneficiaries return to work and provided the ability to waive rules around eligibility and benefit levels for beneficiaries that return to work (Martinez et al., 2010). The Youth in Transition Demonstration (YTD) began in 2003 by the Social Security Administration. The YTD was designed to serve youth with disabilities ages 14 to 25 in 6 project sites across the 5 states - Colorado, Florida, Maryland, New York (Bronx and Erie), and West Virginia - to help them become economically self-sufficient as they were transitioning to adulthood. This demonstration project included waivers to the current SSI rules so that younger participants could continue to access SSI as they gained earnings. These waivers allow:

1. Student Earned Income Exclusions regardless of age while in school;
2. Earned Income Exclusions of $65 plus $3 of every $4 earned;
3. Individual Development Accounts to save earnings plus funds from government and local providers;
4. Plans for Achieving Self-Support for career exploration and post-secondary education; and
5. Benefits to continue regardless of Continuing Disability Reviews and Age 18 Medical Redetermination results.

By 2008 the projects were narrowed down to 6 random assignment sites in 5 states instead of 10 sites in 8 states. Youth were eligible for the program if they were receiving SSI or SSDI (Fraker, 2013). One site included youth that were not currently on benefits, but were at risk of receiving benefits after age 18. The demonstration funded projects to set up coordinated service delivery systems (Green et al., 2005). All 6 random assignment sites completed their YTD participation and services as of March 2012. Currently SSA is evaluating the impacts and a final report will be published in 2014. YTD programs had some flexibility in how to implement the program and with what service providers to partner with. YTD was built on NCWD/Youth's *Guideposts for Success* and required to include 6 components: individual work-based experiences, youth empowerment, family supports, system linkages, social and health services, and benefits counseling (Luecking & Wittenburg, 2009). As an example, California's Bridges to Youth Self-Sufficiency operated in seven school districts across the state and provided a benefits counselor and service coordinator. The program recruited youth from schools and also received referrals from community partners. The program provided employment and benefit counseling, work incentives, job developing and placement, and service coordination (Camacho & Hemmeter, 2013).

Mississippi's Model Youth Transition Innovation also recruited youth (ages 10 to 22) with disabilities from school districts and trained teachers in "individual discovery techniques and customized employment approaches" (p. 62). The program also included Individual Development Accounts. Services were varied based on the age group of the participants. As early as age 10, students received help with planning for future plans. Those ages 14 to 18 received help on developing employment plans. Youth ages 19 to 21 received help with developing vocational profiles and a benefits analysis. For youth ages 22-25, services were provided on an as-needed basis (Camacho & Hemmeter, 2013). Both the California and the Mississippi YTD sites were not selected to be one of the random assignment evaluation sites.

As part of the YTD evaluation, data was collected 12 months post random assignment from all 6 random assignment sites. These early results showed no impacts on employment, income, or high school completion at the Career Transition Program (CTP). Results showed that CTP was no more or less effective than programs and services available to control group members at improving outcomes (Fraker et al., 2012a). In other programs (West Virginia; Colorado; New York City; Erie County, New York) youth who had participated in the program were more likely to use employment support services. The West Virginia and New York participants were more likely to have been employed for earnings than those who did not receive the intervention. However, the programs did not have impacts in enrolling in school or helping participants complete high school in one year after the intervention (Fraker et al. 2011a; Fraker et al., 2011b; Fraker et al., 2011c; Fraker et al., 2012b). Currently, 36-month post random assignment survey data is being collected.

Juvenile Justice

Youth with disabilities who are involved with the juvenile justice system likely face more challenges to successful transition into adult life than their peers. They have to "make up" for any opportunities lost because of their confinement and may have continued restrictions on their activities because of parole. In addition, they have to deal with the challenges that likely led them to be involved with the justice system in the first place, including poverty, lack of positive social support, and inability to function in the mainstream. While incarcerated, they are eligible to access the same transition services as their non-justice involved peers, but it may be more difficult; after release their criminal history may be a serious barrier to receiving services.

Still, it is vitally important to keep young offenders engaged and on the path to self-sufficient adulthood immediately at the point of transition back to the community. Formerly incarcerated youth with disabilities who were working or going to school during their first six months post-release are 3.2 times less likely to return to custody, and 2.5 times more likely to remain working or enrolled in school 12 months post-release (Unruh, Waintrap, Canter & Smith, 2009).

For these youth, "transition" can have multiple meanings – in addition to the transition to adulthood and adult disability services, they are making the transition "from the community to a correctional setting, from one correctional setting to another, or from a correctional setting to post-incarceration activities including public or alternative education, vocational training, integrated employment (including supported employment), continuing education, adult services, independent living, or community participation" (Clark, Mathur & Helding, 2011). In many cases, making a successful transition from incarceration back into the community and avoiding recidivism is a pre-determinant of successful transition to adulthood (Baltodano, Mathur & Rutherford, 2005).

According to estimates from the Annie E. Casey Foundation and the Urban Institute, 400,000 youth cycle through juvenile detention centers each year, and approximately 200,000 youth under the age of 24 are released from juvenile correctional facilities or state and Federal prisons (Kluss, 2012). Estimates of the prevalence of disability among this population vary. The National Disability Rights Network (2012) estimates that 70 percent of the juvenile justice system population have disabilities, including psychiatric, mental health, sensory, and intellectual disabilities as well as co-occurring disorders. Another estimate places the annual number of youth arrested at about 2.2 million and incarcerated at 110,000, of which between 65-70 percent have at least one diagnosable mental health disorder and 60 percent meet the criteria for three or more disorders (Unruh, Waintrap, Canter & Smith, 2009).

The U.S. Department of Education's Office of Special Education Programs reported a conservative estimate of the prevalence of disabilities among school-age children in the juvenile justice system as 32 percent in 2000 (Stenhjem, 2005). The National Collaborative on Workforce & Disability for Youth estimated in 2008 that over one-third of the 144,000 youth committed to out-of-home placements (e.g., secure care facilities) each year are provided with special education services. The percentage of committed youth receiving special education services varies by state, ranging from 9.1 percent to 77.5 percent, and the most common diagnoses among youth involved in the juvenile justice system are emotional disturbances (47.4 percent) and learning disabilities (38 percent) (Gagnon & Richards, 2008).

Federal support for state-run juvenile justice facilities and programs is authorized by the Juvenile Justice and Delinquency Prevention Act (JJDPA) of 1974, P.L. 93-415. The legislation has four areas of compliance for states:

- Offenders whose crimes would not be punishable by imprisonment if they were adults (e.g., truancy) shall not be institutionalized;
- Youth shall not be held in correctional facilities with adults;
- Youth shall be separated from adult prisoners; and
- States shall work to address the disproportionate imprisonment of minority offenders.

Three grant programs the JJDPA authorizes are the Juvenile Justice and Delinquency Prevention State Formula Grants, the Title V Community Prevention Incentive Grants, and the Safe Schools / Healthy Students program, which is jointly authorized by JJDPA, the Safe and Drug-Free Schools and Communities Act, and the Public Health Services Act (Koyanagi, 2012).

Juvenile Justice and Delinquency Prevention State Formula Grants. These grants are allocated to states for local pass-through for delinquency prevention programs. They can support a wide range of programs depending on the state plan, which may or may not include programming targeted to TAY with disabilities (Bazelon, 2008d).

Community Prevention Incentive Grants. This program funds community-based delinquency prevention efforts for at-risk youth and their families, which must be operated as collaboration between local agencies. Treatment for mental health issues is a specifically authorized activity, resulting in collaborative efforts between juvenile justice and mental health agencies. Programming for TAY is allowable, but not prioritized (Bazelon, 2008d).

Safe Schools / Healthy Students. This program encourages local education agencies to collaborate with local mental health, law enforcement, and juvenile justice agencies to provide pro-social services for children, youth, and their families. It supports coordinated, comprehensive activities for this population, including mental health services and behavioral, social, and emotional supports with the goal of developing skills and emotional resilience for positive mental health and social outcomes. However, the program does not specifically target TAY or youth with disabilities, and does not specifically address transition skills (Koyanagi, 2012).

Individuals with Disabilities Education Act. For youth with disabilities in confinement, the Individuals with Disabilities Education Act (IDEA) was the major driving force for equal access to educational opportunities. Under IDEA, Part B, youth under age 18 incarcerated in a juvenile facility – and in many cases youth under age 22 in adult institutions – are entitled to a free, appropriate, public education. An exception is youth in adult facilities who did not have an Individualized Education Program (IEP) in place prior to their conviction (Leone & Weinberg, 2010). As with other youth served under IDEA, starting at age 16, IEPs must include goals and services for transition (Office of Special Education Programs, 2007). Thus, according to the National Center on Education, Disability, and Juvenile Justice, effective special education curricula for TAY with disabilities involved with the juvenile justice system will include transition skills such as functional academic, social, and daily living skills (Carney, n.d.).

No Child Left Behind (NCLB) Act, Title I, Part D: Neglected, Delinquent, or At-Risk Youth. Additionally in the realm of education, the NCLB Title I, Part D addresses the needs of youth who are imprisoned, including transition-related needs, to continue their education or achieve employment (Subpart 1, Section 1418). It encourages collaboration and record sharing between correctional facilities and state educational agencies (Leone & Weinberg, 2010). Allowable uses of funds include counseling, psychological, and social work services; services of in-school advocates to act on behalf of individual children and youth who are neglected or delinquent; tutoring and mentoring; reentry orientation programs, including transition centers and reentry centers in high schools; instruction and training at alternative schools and learning centers; and parental involvement activities and parent counseling (U.S. Department of Education, 2006).

Behavioral Health

The mental health care system provides necessary treatment and support to many youth and adults living with disabilities, particularly those with emotional and behavioral disorders. For adolescents and transition-aged youth, experts in recovery-oriented care list the most important services and supports provided by the mental health care system as:

- Ensuring ongoing family involvement;
- Providing linkage to services;
- Assuring that the range of services and supports address multiple domains in a young person's life;
- Including services that foster social connectedness;
- Providing specialized recovery supports; and
- Providing therapeutic/clinical interventions (Cavanaugh, 2009).

While many of these services might be important at any stage of life, they are critically important during the transition to adulthood, a time when the youth's connection(s) to other institutions (school, family, work) are likely to change.

During this time, mental health services become more needed. In 2008, Kathleen J. Pottick and colleagues (2008) observed a 47 percent decline in utilization of mental health services around the age of transition, but pointed out that this decrease at the age of emancipation "does not align with the fact that young adulthood heralds an increase in the prevalence of psychiatric disorders, reflected in a marked rise in the occurrence of substance use disorders and a peak in the onset of mood disorders and schizophrenia."

According to data from the 2011 National Survey on Drug Use and Health, 29.8 percent of TAY in the U.S. (about 10.1 million) have a mental health condition, with 7.6 percent considered as having a serious mental health issue (Center for Behavioral Health Statistics and Quality, 2012). The Substance Abuse and Mental Health Service Administration (SAMHSA) reports that "of all long-lasting health conditions, mental health disorders produce the greatest disability within this age group" (SAMHSA, 2013). Yet, this age group is also less likely to receive mental health services than population cohorts immediately younger or older: 11.4 percent of TAY receive mental health services, compared to 14.9 percent of 26 to 49 year-olds and approximately 26 percent of 16 to 17 year-olds (Center for Behavioral Health Statistics and Quality, 2012). These service utilization rates foreshadow some of the challenges that the mental health care system has in helping youth with disabilities successfully transition to adulthood, primarily the challenge in transitioning from youth-oriented services to adult-oriented services because of differences in illness definition, insurance coverage, and service availability between the systems.

Like the Juvenile Justice system, the Mental Health system in the United States is extremely decentralized, with service provision decisions being led by the states. The Federal government provides funding (Medicaid, Mental Health Block Grants) for mental health services, but is not prescriptive with programming, and thus it is hard to identify Federal-level programs that address transition needs in particular. Some SAMHSA special initiatives, such as the current Children's Mental Health Initiative, come closer to directly supporting transition services.

Medicaid. Medicaid is the largest source of funding for mental health services in the United States. In 2008, 52 percent of state mental health agency funds were from state and Federal Medicaid sources (Bazelon, 2011). As noted above in the section on Social Security programs, Medicaid provides for a variety of transition services for TAY with disabilities.

Mental Health Block Grant (MHBG). The Center for Mental Health Services awards block grant funds to states to pass through to local community mental health programs. The funds are flexible and can be used to serve TAY who meet the illness eligibility criteria. Community-based services that can be included in state MHBG plans include rehabilitation; employment; housing; education; substance abuse services; medical and dental care; services provided by local school systems under IDEA; and other support services (Bazelon Center for Mental Health Law, 2008b). A 2007 analysis found that 22 states had initiatives to better serve youth in transition funded with MHBG dollars, but 11 states still specifically listed services for TAY as an unmet need for persons with mental illness (NASMHPD, 2007).

Comprehensive Community Mental Health Services for Children and Their Families Program (also called the Children's Mental Health Initiative or CMHI) is a program of the Center for Mental Health Services that awards funds to states and local communities to improve the coordination of services for children and youth up to age 21 with serious emotional disturbance and their families. It is driven by a system of care philosophy with a central focus on providing services that are individualized, strengths-based, and evidence-informed. In 2010, 7.0 percent of CMHI caregivers reported that their participating children had received transition services within the first 12 months of participation in CMHI. However, other transition-related services were more highly reported, including individual therapy (89.8 percent), assessment or evaluation (82.9 percent), case management (90.0 percent), receipt of flexible funds for expenses (42.7 percent), and vocational training (8.8 percent) (Center for Mental Health Services, 2010).

Substance Abuse Prevention and Treatment (SAPT) Block Grant. SAPT is a SAMHSA block grant administered by the Center for Substance Abuse Treatment, giving states funds to plan and execute activities to prevent and treat substance abuse. TAY are not a focus population, though they may be served (Bazelon, 2008c).

Workforce Investment

The workforce system helps TAY through a variety of programs aimed at promoting employment. Similar to the VR system, there is considerable variation across the country in how workforce agencies are serving TAY. The hallmark of the Workforce Investment System is American Job Centers, where individuals, including youth, can receive a variety of services related to employment, education, and job training. American Job Centers also provide access to vocational rehabilitation programs for people with disabilities. The workforce system also includes provisions so that youth with disabilities can participate.[8] Additionally, Department of Labor programs, such as Job Corps and YouthBuild, while not specifically focused on youth with disabilities, also serve this population. Data from the NLTS-2 show that 40 percent of youth with disabilities are not working, but around half were looking for paid employment. Of those who were employed, 55 percent found their employment without assistance and 45 percent received help of some kind – most of which were from a friend or acquaintance. Around 8 percent received help from an employment agency and 4 percent from an individual at their school (Newman et al., 2011).

The WIA system served around 7 million adults in 2012, 228,278 youth through the WIA Youth program, and 25,631 through YouthBuild. The placement rate in employment or education for the WIA Youth program was 62.4 percent; the degree/certificate attainment rate was 64.8 percent; and the percentage of students achieving literacy or numeracy of one Adult Basic Education (ABE) level was 48.3 percent (US Department of Labor, 2013). Due to data collection differences across WIA American Job Centers, it is difficult to discern how many youth with disabilities are served. In a study of 6 WIA American Job Centers in the early 2000s, around 27 percent of the population served were youth ages 5 to 24 years old (Kaufman et al., 2005).

The National Collaborative on Workforce & Disability for Youth reviewed the Workforce Investment Act (WIA) data in 2007 (July 2007 to June 2008) and found that 13.8 percent of youth served under WIA services reported having a disability. Additionally, 62.3 percent of all youth served were placed in employment or education, and the percentage was similar for youth with disabilities (61.4 percent). In terms of attaining a degree, 56.8 percent of all youth served attained a degree or certificate, and 59.1 percent of youth with disabilities attained a degree or certificate. Thus, the averages for youth with disabilities were similar to the general population (National Collaborative on Workforce & Disability for Youth, 2008). The Job Corps program services around 62,000 youth a year. Between 2002 and 2006, 14,386 students entered YouthBuild (specific data on participants with disabilities were unavailable) (Lynn & Mack, 2008).

---

8 Information retrieved from the PACER Center's website: http://www.pacer.org/tatra/resources/workforcewia.asp.

American Job Centers. American Job Centers offer a range of services to benefit TAY with disabilities. The WIA offers funding for youth development to help youth 14 to 21 prepare for postsecondary education and/ or employment. WIA eligibility is based on four categories: one of which is "in need for help completing an educational program or security and holding a job." Therefore, funds can be used to serve TAY with disability-related barriers to employment. WIA serves youth through American Job Centers to provide educational and employment services (Koball, 2011). Services can include assistance to access postsecondary education and employment, mentoring, training, continued services, incentives for achievement, and building leaders and promoting community service opportunities (Koyanagi & Alfano, 2012).

The National Collaborative on Workforce and Disability for Youth reviewed how youth can access workforce development and other work support programs. Youth can enter the workforce system through a variety of programs, including community-based organizations, foster care, juvenile justice, mental health, social security, special education, vocational rehabilitation, and WIA Youth Services (Podmostko, 2007).

Apprenticeship. The Department of Labor's Office of Apprenticeship Services administers apprenticeship programs. According to the Registered Apprenticeship Partners Information Data System (RAPIDS), in Fiscal Year 2013, there were 56,370 active youth apprentices ages 16-24 in the 25 states managed by Department of Labor staff. There are obstacles for youth with disabilities in accessing apprenticeship, and authors recommend that programs offer youth the opportunity for apprenticeship, such as YouthBuild and Job Corps. Many apprenticeship opportunities are in construction, and the authors note that there is little effort to help youth with disabilities to consider construction as an industry, and also to help inform and change perceptions of construction employers so that youth with disabilities can perform in it. The authors recommend trying to enhance employer participation in apprenticeship programs, especially in construction trades, through targeted outreach to these employers (Lynn & Mack, 2008).

Job Corps. Job Corps also helps provide education and training for economically disadvantaged youth (16 to 24) (Koball, 2011). The WIA authorizes discretionary funds to private companies to operate Job Corps Centers. The Centers provide education and training programs to promote career development and to help participants access and maintain employment (Koyanagi & Alfano, 2012). The Job Corps program services around 62,000 youth a year in a residential program across 122 Job Corps Centers. Each region has a disability coordinator to serve enrolled students with disabilities (Lynn & Mack, 2008).

YouthBuild. The YouthBuild program is funded through the Department of Labor's Employment and Training Administration and provides full time programs for youth ages 16 to 24 (Lynn & Mack, 2008). The program is funded through discretionary grants to public or private nonprofits. YouthBuild participants are currently not enrolled in school, and they must also meet one other criteria for eligibility, including being low-income, aging out of foster care, having a disability, etc. (Koyanagi & Alfano, 2012). YouthBuild services include helping student complete their high school education, counseling to access postsecondary education, occupational training, and on-the-job training, and internship opportunities (Koyanagi & Alfano, 2012).

IV. Challenges and Barriers to Serving Youth with Disabilities

This section describes the challenges and barriers to serving TAY with disabilities according to each system. There is a wide range of challenges that are system-specific, but also overlap as is discussed in the next section where common themes are identified.

Vocational Rehabilitation

The literature showed the challenges serving TAY with disabilities through VR include:
- Low Levels of Participation in VR Programs
- Wide Variation Across the Country in VR Programs
- Challenges to Developing National Standards for TAY in VR
- Lack of Research on VR Services for TAY
- Lack of Effective Collaboration with Other Agencies
- Ineffective State and Local Interagency Agreements
- Identification and Referral Barriers

Each of these barriers and the cited literature are discussed in more detail below.

Low Levels of Participation in Vocational Rehabilitation Programs. Using the NLTS-2, Grigal, Hart, and Migliore (2011) found that students with intellectual disabilities (ID) had less positive outcomes than those with other disabilities in terms of attending postsecondary education and also with employment. There were significant differences between students with ID and other disabilities in use of vocational rehabilitation – although low levels of vocational rehabilitation participation existed across both groups (32 percent ID; 24 percent other). Carter and colleagues (2010) also cite that participation was low among TAY with disabilities in accessing career development activities.

Wide Variation Across the Country in VR Programs. Honeycutt and colleagues (2013) argued that "VR agencies have some latitude in determining the services they provide and the clientele they serve, resulting in state-level variation in VR program services, staffing, and expertise for youth with disabilities" (Honeycutt et al., 2013). There is also wide variation in the education level of applicants for VR services. Honeycutt attributes variation to the extent VR agencies coordinate with the education system as some states receive most referrals from primary or secondary schools (like Maine), but others receive referrals after youth have left secondary schooling (like Utah) (Honeycutt et al., 2013).

Challenges to Developing National Standards for TAY in VR. Because the wide range of VR programs across the country is a challenge; one recommendation made was for RSA is to develop national standards, which will be discussed in the recommendation section. Yet, there are challenges to such an approach. For example, to develop employment measures it is necessary to keep state characteristics into account. It is also important to possibly categorize the types of youth being served, like "youth who are in school when they apply for services versus those who have left secondary education, youth receiving SSI benefits or who have more severe disabilities, and youth in postsecondary education programs" (Honeycutt et al., 2013).

Lack of Research on VR Programs for TAY. There has been scarce research on vocational rehabilitation programs for youth, focusing on a small subset of the population with the inability to make comparisons across the population's outcomes (Honeycutt et al., 2013). The National Council on Disability (2008) cites that there has not been prior work that shows the effectiveness of VR on employment outcomes for transition age youth with rigorous evaluation design.

Lack of Effective Collaboration with Other Agencies. The NCD (2008) report documented that VR regularly partners with special education and postsecondary institutions. But, data also show that there are problems with the effectiveness of such collaboration due to the "lack of personnel, service unit credit policies, and dedicated transition units in local rehabilitation agencies" (National Council on Disability, 2008).

Ineffective State and Local Interagency Agreements. Barriers include that some interagency agreements "overestimate the capacity of the VR agency to fully implement all of the procedures, processes, and services," and there is no oversight to make sure that the processes identified in the agreements are completed. Additionally, such agreements are not specific in terms of roles and responsibilities (The Study Group, 2007).

Identification and Referral Barriers. The Study Group (2007) identified that some TAY who may be eligible for VR are not referred into VR. Additionally, some local school staff may not fully understand VR in order to make referrals for TAY to the VR agency. Additionally, getting the buy-in from families is also difficult. VR agencies often have financial limitations which can make it difficult to attend transition planning meetings and provide services for youth while they are still in high school (The Study Group, 2007).

Social Security

The literature showed the challenges serving TAY with disabilities in the Social Security System include:
- Disincentives to Work
- Disability Determination and Policy Consistency
- Challenges to Success in Job Attachment
- Increasing Successful Work Attempts
- Accessing Social Security Benefits
- Health Insurance Discontinuity

Each of these barriers and the cited literature are discussed in more detail below.

Disincentives to Enter, Re-enter, and Maintain Employment. One of the biggest challenges with having youth access employment while receiving Social Security benefits is the disincentive to work for fear of losing benefits (Green et al., 2005; O'Day, 2012). Green and colleagues (2005) cite that "the financial disincentives to work and earn income along with the lack of adequate employment training and placement services were, and continue to be, significant barriers to employment." Thus, youth may not feel compelled to access employment because they may lose their benefits as their earned income increases. As beneficiaries have changes in their income or living situation, benefit eligibility levels might change. O'Leary and colleagues also note that if beneficiaries access employment, they are often in "unstable circumstances" and "changes in earnings can affect eligibility for benefits, potentially leading to income instability and changes in living arrangements; also, the physical and mental rigors of employment might exacerbate existing health conditions" (O'Leary, Livermore, & Stapleton, 2011).

Challenges to Success in Job Attachment. Additionally, from the Ticket to Work evaluation, findings reveal that beneficiaries that do attempt to return to work have unstable support systems in place. Employment and working a job may aggravate existing mental and physical health conditions (O'Leary, Livermore, & Stapleton, 2011). Thus, a challenge in developing a policy to increase successful work attempts is that "such policies and programs may lead to substantially greater expenditures. Future expansion of the number of TTW users is likely to mean providing VR or EN services for some beneficiaries who would have left the disability rolls even without receiving such services. Offsetting reductions in benefit costs for such users will materialize only if they spend more time off the rolls than they otherwise would have" (O'Leary, Livermore, & Stapleton, 2011).

Another challenge includes context and environmental factors, specifically, O'Leary and colleagues (2011) cite factors such as the ability/interest of employers to hire people with disabilities, access to health care, transportation, family issues, and work incentives of other social programs (O'Leary, Livermore & Stapleton, 2011). Additional findings as part of the Ticket to Work Program from the 2004 National Beneficiary Survey, a nationally representative survey of SS disability beneficiaries, revealed that beneficiaries continue to face challenges to employment, such as low levels of education, poverty, lack of transportation, inaccessible workplaces, and also "discouragement from work either by others or through their own experiences" (Livermore, Goodman, & Wright, 2007).

Increasing Successful Work Attempts. O'Leary and colleagues cite that in order to increase work attempts for social security beneficiaries, there are two major challenges. Specifically, by expanding TTW, some providers may be offering services to beneficiaries who may have been able to attach to the labor market without services. And, a beneficiary's success in achieving gainful employment may be outside of the SSA's control due to environmental factors that may influence employment outcomes (O'Leary, Livermore, & Stapleton, 2011). A challenge in increasing successful work attempts by SSI-eligible transition age youth may also be limited by family incomes and costly health care needs (Davies et al., 2009).

Accessing Social Security Benefits. In serving this population as a whole, some researchers argue that certain types of disabilities experience more challenges than others to access social security benefits. In a research article focused on the experiences of child SSI beneficiaries when they receive their redetermination of adult benefits at age 18, it was found that youth with mental or behavioral disorders were less like to receive SSI at age 19, and certain non-health factors, such as education, employment, and social indicators, also impacted the likelihood of receiving benefits as an adult (Hemmeter, Kauff, & Wittenburg, 2009).

Health Insurance Discontinuity. When they lose SSI coverage because of age cutoffs or differing illness definitions between the child and adult systems, TAY with disabilities can also lose Medicaid coverage. Adolescent consumers may stop being eligible for Medicaid-covered care at age 18, 19, 20, or 21, depending on the state. These age limitations are based on bureaucratic definitions of adulthood, and thus do not take into account factors such as individuals' developmental readiness to assume new responsibilities (Pottick et al., 2008; Manteuffel, Stephens, Sondheimer & Fisher, 2008). Pullman et al. (2010) found that "aging-out of Medicaid coverage…appeared to be strongly related to disenrollment as there were significant periods of disenrollment near individuals' 18th and 19th birthdays," but noted that need for care does not end promptly with one's end of eligibility. Medicaid eligibility also has interactions with eligibility for other public assistance programs such as Temporary Assistance for Needy Families (TANF). For example, low-income females who become mothers before the age of transition may be able stay on Medicaid as TANF parent participants, while low-income males who qualified for Medicaid as TANF child participants may lose coverage when they move off TANF at age 18 (Pullman, 2010). In 2002, it was estimated that "74 percent of children on Medicaid with potentially disabling medical conditions such as severe asthma, diabetes, HIV, cancer, and cystic fibrosis meet Medicaid eligibility criteria based on their age and family income, but do not meet the disability standards required for receipt of SSI" (Williams & Tolbert, 2007), meaning they would lose health coverage when they pass the age limit.

Juvenile Justice

The literature showed the challenges serving TAY with disabilities in juvenile justice include:

- Focus on Punishment Rather than Rehabilitation
- Fragmentation of Services
- Post Release Barriers
- Lack Support of Family and Home Life
- Lack of Transition Training Within the Juvenile Justice System

Each of these barriers and the cited literature are discussed in more detail below.

Focus on Punishment rather than Rehabilitation. The policy paradigm in the U.S. juvenile and criminal justice systems swings between one focused on "rehabilitation and reintegration" to one more focused on "deterrence and punishment" (Altschuler, 2005). The 2002 reauthorization of the Juvenile Justice and Delinquency Prevention Act reflected a shift to the latter (Nuñez-Neto, 2007). With this approach comes decreased funding for job training, drug counseling, housing assistance, and similar services which are considered key components of transition assistance (Altschuler, 2005). There is evidence that states are looking to shift this paradigm back to one of treatment and support, but substantive changes to the juvenile justice system would require changing organizational culture and challenging societal expectation for corrections (Lipsey, Howell, Kelly, Chapman & Carver, 2010).

Fragmentation of Services. When such services are available to youth within the juvenile justice system, they are often uncoordinated. "Services are fragmented as a result of each agency having individual eligibility criteria, case plans, records, and lack of support to communicate or coordinate with other agencies. Although the same needs for a high-risk youth may be identified by all agencies, agencies may view what is needed differently. This can lead to duplication of services, multiple assessments, and refusal of new services by the family due to negative past experiences" (Stenhjem, 2005). Further challenges to collaboration between systems include divergent case management approaches, a lack of collaborative funding strategies, and a perceived gap in the mission of each agency as well as unclear lines of authority and responsibility and strained budgets for service provision (Altschuler, Stangler, Berkley & Burton, 2009; Altschuler, 2005). A specific, often-cited example of poor systems coordination that leads to duplicative and inappropriate services is the difficulty obtaining previous educational records for incarcerated youth (Leone, & Weinberg, 2010).

In addition, services may become fragmented at the time of release for youth who have been incarcerated. For example, detention facility staff have incentive to focus on short-term post-release arrangements instead of long term solutions for successful transition, which may require more coordination (Hanger 2008). Additionally, institutional corrections and juvenile probations systems may be uncoordinated in their goals and policies; for example, restrictive leave policies interfering with the job search process (Altschuler, 2005; Hanger, 2008). This is especially perilous for youth who are transitioning to adulthood and adult services at the same time as they are transitioning back into the community, for they have to meet societal expectations of adults without having had the opportunity to learn and practice skills necessary for adulthood (Unruh, Povenmire-Kirk & Yamamoto, 2009; Muller, 2011).

Post Release Barriers. Youth who are no longer in custody may face residual barriers. Because of their involvement with the justice system, they may be ineligible for assistance necessary for successful transition, including housing assistance and vocational training. Furthermore, their employability is compromised by their record, both from being legally disqualified from some professions and from stigma (Altschuler, 2005; Unruh, Povenmire-Kirk & Yamamoto, 2009). These realities challenge the ex-offender's sense of social inclusion and ability to build resilience (Altschuler, 2005).

Lack Support of Family and Home Life. Youth transitioning back to the community may have more urgent needs than youth who had lived with their families. Families often provide basic supports from which an adolescent can transition into adulthood. But if the formerly incarcerated youth has no welcoming or healthy family to go home to, their need for basic supports like housing is imminent. They also have family life functioning to learn about - youth who have been institutionalized may not have had an opportunity to learn independent living skills like cleaning clothes, managing money, and cooking in a family environment (Unruh, Povenmire-Kirk & Yamamoto, 2009).

Lack of Transition Training within the Juvenile Justice System. Providing professional development and specialized transition training for service providers has not been a priority for the juvenile justice system (Leone & Weinberg, 2010).

Behavioral Health

The literature showed the challenges serving TAY with disabilities in the mental health system include:
- Insurance and Service Discontinuity
- Medicaid Waiver Restrictions
- Segregated Child and Adult Systems
- Scarcity of Appropriate Services
- Confidentiality Barriers to Family Participation

Each of these barriers and the cited literature are discussed in more detail below.

Insurance and Service Discontinuity. Service eligibility often depends on one's diagnosis. Mental health and substance use disorders are defined and covered differently for children than for adults, meaning some individuals may stop being covered as an adult for an illness that was covered as a child (Davis & Sondheimer, 2005; Pottick et al., 2008; Heflinger, 2008; Manteuffel, Stephens, Sondheimer & Fisher, 2008; Jivanlee & Kruzich, 2011). This is a critical problem with the Federal Mental Health Block Grants (MHBG) (Davis & Koyanagi, 2005). It is also a problem for Medicaid (see discussion below) since Medicaid is a significant source of funding for state mental health agencies Medicaid accounted for 48 percent of this funding in 2010 (state and Federal combined) (NASMHPD, 2012).

Medicaid Waiver Restrictions. While Medicaid waivers are a source of funding for innovative and promising approaches to serving TAY, even the waivers have some restrictions that prevent innovation, such as not funding services for youth with an IQ above 70 or therapy services for young people with developmental disabilities. In general, funding is often quite limited in scope, requiring programs to braid funds in order to offer comprehensive services (Davis, 2010).

Segregated Child and Adult Systems. Beyond the issue of different illness definitions in the child and adult state mental health systems, there are other barriers that having two separate systems poses for delivering quality transition services. The formal mechanisms for communication between these systems are limited, and each system has its own organizational culture. For example, the child mental health system is accustomed to involving the family in care decisions, coordinating with other service systems, and remaining aware of consumer's developmental needs, while the adult system focuses on the individual and tends to be less supportive and rehabilitative (Davis, n.d.). Moreover, neither system views TAY as a primary target population, and state mental health policy and funding often does not support shared planning or coordination between the two systems (Pottick et al., 2008; Bazelon, 2008). Finally, on a logistical level, transitioning from one system to another means changing staff (e.g., case managers, therapists) and often service site locations (Helfinger, 2008). These challenges are compounded by the fact that there are no special advocates or case managers to help consumers and their families navigate (Heflinger, 2008; Manteuffel, Stephens, Sondheimer & Fisher, 2008). Another realm of system segregation that must be coordinated is between state mental health and substance abuse agencies (S. Green, personal communication, November 19, 2013).

Scarcity of Appropriate Services. The availability and service capacity of transition service providers in the child and adult mental health systems varies across the country. A survey of state mental health program administrators in 2005 uncovered that 12 states have no transition services offered anywhere in the state by child mental health services (Davis & Sondheimer, 2005). The scarcity is even more widespread according to a 2006 study of both youth and adult state mental health systems which found that "one-quarter of child state mental health systems and one-half of adult state mental health systems offered no transition services, and few provided any kind of transition service at more than one site. Most types of transition services were available in less than 20 percent of the states" (Davis, Geller & Hunt, 2006). Furthermore, this study found that services had uneven geographic distribution within states (Davis, Geller & Hunt, 2006).

Accessing age-appropriate transition services may be even more challenging for youth with multiple disabilities. "Programs serving young people with dual diagnoses fall into two groups (a) those designed for individuals with dual diagnoses, some of them in the young adult age range, and (b) those serving young people in transition with mental health challenges, a few of whom also have a developmental disability" (Davis, Jivanjee & Koroloff, 2010).

Accessing age-appropriate transition services may also be more difficult for youth who live in rural areas. Heflinger & Hoffman (2009) found that rural youth were approximately 10 percent more likely to possess multiple risk factors for transition difficulties (e.g., having a serious emotional disturbances, at risk of or in foster care/state custody, intensive or frequent mental health services usage) than their urban counterparts, but have fewer services available to them, particularly youth in rural correctional facilities.

Confidentiality Barriers to Family Participation. Once an individual does reach adulthood, doctor-patient confidentiality issues may pose a barrier to involving parents and family members in transition planning (Jivanlee & Kruzich, 2011), which is recognized throughout transition planning models as a crucial practice.

Workforce Investment

The literature showed the challenges serving TAY with disabilities in the Workforce Investment system include:
- Difficulty with System Change and Lack of Multifaceted, Intense Programming
- Insufficient Staff Training and Funding
- Eligibility and Accessibility
- Difficulty with Program Compliance
- Operating with Budget Cuts
- WIA Reauthorization

Each of these barriers and the cited literature are discussed in more detail below.

Difficulty with System Change and Lack of Multifaceted, Intense Programming. The U.S. Department of Labor Office of Disability Employment Policy (ODEP) conducted a demonstration program for customized employment in American Job Centers, formerly One-Stop Career Centers. The program reported positive outcomes of individuals who participated in the program in the areas of services received and employment such as job maintenance and average wage earnings above minimum wage. During the program, system change was critical to program success, and sustaining such change can be a challenge. However, partnerships with a broad range of local and state agencies can help promote and sustain systems change (Elinson et al., 2008). While youth need tailored services, findings from the demonstration revealed that the understanding of "customized employment" was unclear as some continued to think in a "linear chain of services" as opposed to a suite of services tailored to the individual (Elinson et al., 2008). Additionally, research funded through the Bill and Melinda Gates Foundation showed that vulnerable youth are not likely to voluntarily join programs, and youth need long lasting, multifaceted programming (Bloom, Thompson, & Ivry, 2010).

The GAO 2008 report, entitled Y*oung Adults with Serious Mental Illness: Some States and Federal Agencies are Taking Steps to Address their Transition Challenges*, also cited that WIA youth centers reported that they could not provide the customized support needed for youth with severe mental health disabilities. WIA programming is largely a self-directed pathway for participants, and accommodations for disabilities are made based on self-disclosure. Additionally, there may be a disincentive for agencies to serve the hardest to serve who need long term support due to performance measurement requirements (GAO, 2008; Larson, 2009).

Additionally, Moreno and colleagues cite that TAY with disabilities face challenges to successful transition due to insufficient vocational supports, meaning work-based activities. Youth in high school may not have connections to access work-based, skill building supports (Moreno et al., 2013).

Insufficient Staff Training and Funding. The Next Generation Youth Work Coalition conducted a policy scan of Federal programs for helping youth transition into the workforce, and found that few programs require training of their staff. As the National Collaborative on Workforce and Disability for Youth noted in 2012, "there is no career pathway or cohesive professional development system through which [youth service professionals preparing youth for the transition to adulthood] can receive training and education in core competencies that culminates in a nationally recognized professional certification or degree" (National Collaborative on Workforce & Disability for Youth, 2012). Authors also cite that funding is a challenge as program directors are pressured to use their funds toward direct services instead of providing workforce support to their own workers (Cole & Ferrier, 2009).

Eligibility and Accessibility. The National Collaborative on Workforce and Disability for Youth cite a disconnection when youth are transitioning from accessing child services to then accessing adult services. Some child services end at 18, while others at 22. Specifically, "the adult systems of education, mental health, Social Security, vocational rehabilitation, and workforce development often have different terminology, eligibility requirements, and service options than those of the corresponding youth systems. This disconnect can result in consequences such as termination of services and lost progress in career planning" (Podmostko, 2007).

As part of the ODEP initiative to help American Job Centers meet the needs of people with disabilities, Elinson and colleagues noted that many American Job Centers are not fully accessible for people with disabilities, and accessibility audits and continuous monitoring of progress may help alleviate the situation (Elinson et al., 2008).

Difficulty with Program Compliance. The WIA youth with disabilities study, it was identified that compliance with the performance measures and accountability is a challenge for sites. Sites also stated that the performance measures limit the number of proposals they receive in response to the annual request for proposals (RFP). Additionally, sites were concerned that increasing performance measures would limit youth with disabilities in accessing services, and specifically discourage sites from serving youth who would appear to need additional supports to meet performance measures (Kaufman et al., 2005).

Operating with Budget Cuts. The WIA youth with disabilities study, entitled How Youth with Disabilities are Served through the Workforce Development System: Case Study Research Across Six Sites, also cited that budget cuts had an impact on the ability of WIA Youth programs to provide a comprehensive suite of services. Sites expressed a need to help them streamline service delivery and reduce costs (Kaufman et al., 2005).

WIA Reauthorization. The WIA youth disabilities study sites noted that the lack of WIA reauthorization had caused them to stagnate their processes, rather than developing new policies and procedures, as they anticipate changes when WIA is reauthorized (Kaufman et al., 2005).

V. Recommendations for Enhancing Systems' Capacity

This section describes the recommendations contained in the literature for improving services to TAY with disabilities related to the five systems studied. Some of these recommendations are system-specific and, may overlap. This is discussed in the next section where common themes are identified.

Vocational Rehabilitation

The literature showed the following recommendations for the Vocational Rehabilitation system in enhancing services to TAY with disabilities:

- Enhance Supported Education
- Build Awareness for VR
- Promote VR Programs for TAY
- Integrate VR and Medicaid
- Develop VR Program Standards for TAY
- Increase Cultural Competency
- Involve Family in Career Planning
- Increase Staff Development for TAY
- Enhance VR Counselor Skills
- Improve State LEA and VR Partnerships
- Change VR Policy at Congressional Level
- Change Service Structure at Federal and State Level

Each of these recommendations and the cited literature are discussed in more detail below.

Enhance Supported Education. Entry into education or job training can be an allowable outcome under the Individual Placement and Support (IPS) model, since it aligns with the principle of respecting the client's preferences. Supported education is defined as "supports 'to assist people with psychiatric disabilities to take advantage of skill, career, educational, and inter-personal development opportunities within postsecondary educational environments'" where clinical and vocational services are integrated. Delman and Ellison (2013) suggest that practitioners working with TAY should advocate for supported education for TAY but note challenges in integrating supported education with supported employment. These challenges include the following: adjusting target outcomes to include educational participation, providing specialized training for practitioners in educational coaching, and addressing the financial cost of higher education.

Build Awareness for Vocational Rehabilitation. From a 2010 study, Smith and colleagues recommended using postsecondary education as a way to promote employment outcomes (Smith, Grigal, & Sulewsi, 2012). Conversely, as high school age youth are creating transition plans, vocational rehabilitation counselors can be involved in the planning process. Vocational rehabilitation counselors are involved in transition planning for 30 percent of students with visual impairments and 12 percent for students with emotional disturbances (Koyanagi & Alfano, 2012).

Promote VR Programs for TAY. Youth are an important population served by VR agencies. Honeycutt et al. recommend that in order to promote services received by TAY in VR programs, policymakers should "develop specific standards and indicators for agencies." Such standards, like public monitoring, could help improve outcomes for youth accessing VR services. Additionally, more information is needed to understand what specific agency practices influence successful transition among this population (Honeycutt et al., 2013).

According to the U.S. Department of Education:
> *Section 106 of the Rehabilitation Act of 1973, as amended, already requires that RSA establish evaluation standards and performance indicators for the VR program (see below), and Section 107 of the Rehabilitation Act of 1973, as amended (Act), requires the commissioner of the Rehabilitation Services Administration (RSA)*

to conduct annual reviews and periodic on-site monitoring of programs authorized under Title I of the Act to determine whether a state VR agency is complying substantially with the provisions of its state plan under Section 101 of the Act.

Standards and Indicators Section 106 of the Rehabilitation Act of 1973, as amended, requires the Rehabilitation Services Administration (RSA) to establish evaluation standards and performance indicators for the vocational rehabilitation (VR) program that include outcome and related measures of program performance. Two evaluation standards were published in the Federal Register on Monday, June 5, 2000 (34 CFR Part 361). Each year, state VR agencies must report program performance data to RSA by December 1st (60 days after the end of the fiscal year). RSA has established minimum levels of performance for each performance indicator. State agencies that fail to meet these performance levels must develop a Program Improvement Plan (PIP) outlining specific actions to be taken to improve program performance. RSA also provides technical assistance to those state agencies that perform below the established performance levels. For each Standard and Indicator, separate tables are provided for:

- *General/Combined Agencies (G/C), which are either agencies serving all individuals with disabilities in the state, or agencies serving all individuals with disabilities except those who are blind or visually impaired; and*
- *State Agencies for the Blind (B), which are agencies that provide services only for individuals who are blind or visually impaired. Monitoring, Section 107 of the Rehabilitation Act of 1973, as amended (Act), requires the commissioner of the Rehabilitation Services Administration (RSA) to conduct annual reviews and periodic on-site monitoring of programs authorized under Title I of the Act to determine whether a state VR agency is complying substantially with the provisions of its state plan under Section 101 of the Act and with the Evaluation Standards and Performance Indicators established under Section 106.*[9]

Integrate VR and Medicaid. The American Public Human Services Association (APHSA) provides recommendations to give States flexibility to integrate VR and Medicaid funds, which will help provide incentives for work (APHSA, 2012). Doing so, would allow states to coordinate case management, person-centered planning, and service/resource coordination between VR and Medicaid to ensure optimal use and continuity of resources for TAY.

Develop VR Program Standards for TAY. Honeycutt and colleagues (2013) argue that there are state differences in VR programming for TAY, and "if policymakers want to promote the services the transition-age population receives, they could develop specific standards and indicators for agencies regarding this population." Such standards could help increase the number of youth who receive VR services. The key question, though, is what the agency standards should be. The Rehabilitation Services Administration has general standards for the population service by VR agencies, but none in relation to TAY (Honeycutt et al., 2013). Similarly, Balcazar et al. (2013) recommend that there be a review of what is being done in each state for VR transition programs and that each state VR agency should "conduct a systematic program of future research to identify the characteristics and service needs" for TAY with disabilities.

Increase Cultural Competency. Balcazar and colleagues (2013) found that females had more poor employment outcomes than males, and suggest that "more attention could focus on the potential cultural and behavioral differences that may be relevant to them." Some families may also have "restrictive cultural values about female roles and responsibilities." Additionally, minority males were less likely to enroll in postsecondary education, and it is recommended that counselors become aware of the context by which minority youth with disabilities reside and come from (Balcazar et al., 2013). Gonzalez and colleagues (2011) also show that Native American, African American, and Asian American young adults with learning disabilities have the least success in achieving employment after receiving VR services.

---

9 Information retrieved from the U.S. Department of Education's website: http://www2.ed.gov/rschstat/eval/rehab/standards.html.

Involve Family in Career Planning. In a research brief by the U.S. Department of Education, authors cite that little work has been done on the family's role in the process of helping people with disabilities find employment. Families can often help individuals navigate available services. Families should be involved in planning that can begin as early as middle school. They also recommend defining family broadly to include neighbors and teachers to help build career plans, which can help expand "both the VR counselor's and the family's reach." This also involves helping the family learn how to navigate the system, understanding that families may be protective, and that work might be a disincentive because of losing benefits (Rhodes, 2010).

Increase Staff Development for TAY. There is a need to increase staff development for TAY in vocational rehabilitation agencies to help serve the TAY population with disabilities. Balcazar and colleagues (2013) recommend targeted recruitment and professional development to build counselors to better serve this population. In a study of three Midwest states, Plotner and colleagues found that there is a need to strengthen VR services for transition planning as VR counselors are often not included in VR planning, and one reason for such findings is that VR counselors have limited opportunities for continuing education (Plotner, Trach, & Strauser, 2012). Additionally, Gonzalez and colleagues call for a "greater awareness for government initiatives" by VR counselors as well as future rehabilitation practitioners so that appropriate discussions of benefit counseling are held early in the planning process. The Study Group (2007) cited that VR staff serving TAY do not have the time and resources to attend continuing education and professional development courses.

Enhance VR Counselor Skills. Lindstrom, Kahn, and Lindsey (2013) conducted a literature review to better understand career development for youth with disabilities entering the workforce. In the literature, they cite major barriers to advancing in the labor market. VR counselors can help youth build skills through "strengths based exploration and planning" and by partnering with schools. Counselors can also support youth in exploration about possible careers through work-based instruction and community work experiences. Counselors can serve as advocates for their consumers to help provide employers with information about accommodating people with disabilities (Lindstrom, Kahn, & Lindsey, 2013).

Improve State LEA and VR Partnerships. The Study Group (2007) made a variety of recommendations toward building more effective transition policy which include strengthening the relationship and collaboration between both state and local VR and LEA agencies. Specifically, they argue for the promotion of "state and local interagency agreements as a strategy for enhancing the collaboration between VR and special education programs." Additionally, there is a need to enhance identification and referral procedures and build integrated data systems across agencies (The Study Group, 2007).

Change VR Policy at the Congressional Level. The National Council on Disability (NCD) (2008) provided recommendations for Congress on VR legislation. These recommendations are stated below in the exact wording of the NCD report:

1. *Congress should change existing VR transition legislation and policy to require that VR services be made available to eligible youth no later than three years before an adolescent or young adult exits from secondary education.*
2. *Congress should authorize and allocate sufficient funds to support the development of a multifunctional transition unit in each state VR agency.*
3. *Congress should authorize and mandate the development and implementation of coordinated service delivery approaches, specifically targeted to transitioning youth with disabilities, that are based on the "blending" of funds from VR, special education, postsecondary education, Workforce Investment Act of 1998 (WIA), Veterans Administration, Social Security Administration, and other appropriate funding agencies.*
4. *Congress should mandate that RSA, NIDRR, and state VR agencies conduct rigorous evaluation studies that identify the transition program components that directly correlate with improved employment and postsecondary educational outcomes for transition-age youth.*

5. *Congress should mandate and allocate funds to support the implementation of rigorous evaluation studies designed to establish the efficacy of fully developed transition programs, practices, and policies. (NCD, 2008).*

Change Service Structure at Federal and State Level. The NCD also provides recommendations for the U.S. Department of Education: RSA, NIDRR, OSEP, and State VR Agencies:

1. *RSA, NIDRR, and state VR agencies should develop, implement, and evaluate new service unit policies under which the services provided by VR counselors outside the individualized plan for employment (IPE), such as time spent in collaboration with other agencies, secondary and postsecondary schools, families, etc., are recognized as service units comparable to IPE services.*
2. *RSA, NIDRR, and state VR agencies should design, implement, and evaluate a tiered structure for services delivered by VR counselors working with transition-age youth.*
3. *RSA and state VR agencies should allocate additional staff development resources for the preparation of current and future rehabilitation counselors to meet the needs of transition-age youth, and target recruitment and professional development activities to attract qualified people with disabilities to the field.*
4. *RSA should coordinate its secondary transition efforts with those of other federal and state agencies implementing dropout prevention programs.*
5. *RSA, NIDRR, OSEP, and state VR agencies should collaborate to conduct a comprehensive review of existing VR transition programs, practices, and policies being implemented in each individual state.*
6. *RSA, NIDRR, OSEP, and state VR agencies should conduct a systematic program of future research to identify the characteristics and service needs of transition-age youth with disabilities currently unserved or underserved by VR (NCD, 2008).*

Social Security

The literature showed the following recommendations for the Social Security system in enhancing services for TAY with disabilities:

- Revise Policy to Encourage Employment
- Coordinate Services
- Increase Outreach among Participants and Providers
- Increase Research on State Differences
- Reinstate Social Security Student Benefit

Each of these recommendations and the cited literature are discussed in more detail below.

Revise Policy to Encourage Employment. The Ticket to Work and Work Incentives Improvement Act Advisory Panel recommended that Congress "modernize "the SSA definition of disability, which is used in SSI/SSDI eligibility. The definition currently requires that an individual have a disability, which prevents them from working, which discourages beneficiaries from employment (O'Day & Stapleton, 2009; O'Day, 2012).

Coordinate Services. There is a need to coordinate among programs in the long-term and consider life cycle perspective when making recommendations to better understand long-term outcomes. Specifically, Davies and colleagues state that "coordination between vocational rehabilitation programs for transition-age youth and middle school level special education could lead to enhancing the focus of special education programs on basic skills that are essential for successful labor force entry" (Davies, Rupp, & Wittenburg, 2009). Findings from YTD reveal that successful programs relied on strong partnerships, clear planning (intervention components linked to measureable outcomes), and support services provided in conjunction with employment services (Camacho & Hemmeter, 2013; Martinez, et al., 2010). Additionally, smaller scale programs appeared to be better at serving those with high service needs. Martinez and colleagues (2010) also recommended, "getting to scale often entails operating the same program in multiple, highly dispersed locations with different service environments, economic conditions, and population demographics."

Increase Outreach among Participants and Providers. An evaluation of the TTW program's post-rollout implementation and early impacts showed that outreach could increase program participation. Also, there are little financial incentives for providers to participate in TTW (Thornton et al., 2007). Thornton and colleagues (2007) called for a need to expand the program and build momentum.

Youth present a good opportunity to intervene because unlike adults, they are not "fully entrenched in dependency." The Ticket to Work and Work Incentives Improvement Act Advisory Panel recommended implementing a policy called Transition to Economic Self-Sufficiency (TESS) to help youth ages 14 to 30 gain employment. The TESS program would help provide supports to youth with disabilities between the ages of 14 and 30 and offer work incentives (O'Day & Stapleton, 2009). The Panel recommended the program would help build an investment in youth, as opposed to maintenance. Once participants meet a specified income level, the cash benefits would be reduced on a gradual scale, and it would also help beneficiaries build "Independence Accounts." The TESS demonstration would also help youth access internships and other transition work programs (Ticket to Work and Work Incentives Advisory Panel, 2007).[10]

Increase Research on State Differences. King and Rukh-Kamaa (2013) conducted a study of the SSA's new policy for foster care youth to apply for SSI benefits 90 days before their 18th birthday. They conclude that there is a need to study "how differences in state policies influence SSI application rates" as "state policy determines the amount and funding source of foster care payments, both of which affect an individual's eligibility for SSI" (King & Rukh-Kamaa, 2013).

Reinstate Social Security Student Benefit. The National Academy of Social Insurance argues that the age to receive social security should be raised to age 22 for young adult children of deceased and workers with disabilities who are enrolled in school. Previously, the Social Security "student benefit" was in place starting in 1965, but ended in 1981. By reinstating this benefit, it would help promote higher education among this population as higher education is costly and financial aid hard to come by. The National Academy estimates that the cost of a student benefit would be around 0.07 percent of the taxable payroll over the 75-year horizon (Hertel-Fernandez, 2010).

Juvenile Justice

The literature showed the following recommendations for the juvenile justice system in enhancing services for TAY with disabilities:
- Offer High Quality Transition Programming to Address the Needs of Youth Involved with the Juvenile Justice System
- Improve Cross-System Collaboration
- Create Opportunities for Success in Employment
- Consider the Use of Diversion and Graduated Sanctions to Prevent Youth from Entering the Juvenile Justice System

Each of these recommendations and the cited literature are discussed in more detail below.

Offer High Quality Transition Programming to Address the Needs of Youth Involved with the Juvenile Justice System. In many ways, the transition needs of youth with disabilities involved with the juvenile justice system are the same as their peers. Because these youth experience two types of transition – the transition to adulthood and the transition out of a juvenile care facility – their needs are magnified and their access to services is more restricted. For this reason, services offered via the juvenile justice system have to reach a higher standard. In a review of ten studies that looked for characteristics of successful transition programming, Baltodano, Mathur & Rutherford (2010) identified the following as important for this population:

---

10 The Panel's legislated authority ended on January 17, 2008.

1. **Preplanning for transition.** This recommendation is rooted in a "continuity of care" principle whereby youth can continue to access services after release to build on the skills and knowledge obtained while in the facility (Altschuler, 2005; Chung, 2005; Muller, 2011). For example, in Pennsylvania which is undertaking comprehensive aftercare reform, the goal is for individualized aftercare planning to begin at disposition (sentencing) (Griffin, Steele & Franklin, 2007).

2. **Fostering attitudes of internal control of life events.** This recommendation is echoed by the National Collaborative on Workface and Disability for Youth, which lists one of the specific needs of youth involved with the juvenile justice system as "additional emphasis on self-empowerment through training in self-advocacy, self-esteem, self-reliance, self-determination, and self-sufficiency" (2010).

3. **Encouraging engagement in the months immediately following release from the correctional facility.** A study of the Arizona Detention Transition Project found that providing re-entering offenders with "enhanced" transition services – including vocational assessments, resumes, and transcripts – was associated with a 64 percent decrease in recidivism at 30 days post-release. In addition, providing access to a Transition Specialist resulted in a higher percentage of active Individual Education Plans and Individual Transition Plans among treatment group members, and increases in the amounts and types of transition services provided to youth with disabilities (Nelson, Jolivette, Leone & Mathur, 2010; Clark, Mathur & Helding, 2011).

4. **Establishing positive peer models and influences during transition.** In focus groups held with juvenile offenders, not necessarily ones with disabilities, about the factors that will make their re-entry difficult or smoother, 47 percent of respondents indicated that positive peer engagement could enhance the transition process, by providing support, making school more appealing for its social aspect, and sharing healthy recreational activities (Unruh, Povenmire-Kirk & Yamamoto, 2009).

5. **Providing high-quality education and treatment programs both in corrections and during the transition process.** A catalog of evidence-based and research-based juvenile justice programming is being built, and allowing states to require their use within the system. Broadly, a meta-analysis of 548 controlled studies identified common characteristics among juvenile justice programs effective at reducing subsequent offenses. These include: being rooted in a therapeutic philosophy, specifically offering group counseling and mentoring programs, and replicating the model program with fidelity (Lipsey, Howell, Kelly, Chapman & Carver, 2010).

6. **Addressing gender differences in meeting the unique transition needs of youth.** Because females have a higher school drop-out rate than males, Baltodano, Mathur & Rutherford (2010) argue that they need intensive specialized intervention and rehabilitation programs.

7. **Establishing strong adult mentors to support youth as they make the transition to the community.** Through focus groups with young offenders, 72 percent of respondents indicated that emotional support from members was crucial to making decisions for a positive transition to adulthood (Unruh, Povenmire-Kirk & Yamamoto, 2009). The likelihood that parents will be able to support their children during transition can be enhanced by providing services (e.g., behavioral health, substance abuse treatment) to families as well as the youth offenders (Altschuler, Stangler, Berkley & Burton, 2009). Another source of adult support can be from service professionals. One example of how this approach is being utilized is in Allegheny County, Pennsylvania. Under the state's Juvenile Justice and Delinquency Prevention effort supported by the MacArthur Foundation's Models for Change initiative, Allegheny County justice officials used state-awarded Drug Control and System Improvement funds to hire Education Specialists who visit facilities to monitor educational services to juveniles in placement, assess and enhance the quality of those services, and help coordinate educational transitions at the time of release (Griffin, Steele & Franklin, 2007).

Through other research, the additional recommendations made include:

Improve Cross-System Collaboration. An individual juvenile offender with disabilities may likely be receiving services from the mental health care system, the special education system, and the juvenile justice system itself.

This creates the potential for three treatment plans to follow and, duplicative and uncoordinated services. Coordinating treatment, planning, and case management across systems would result in more streamlined service and better outcomes (Nelson, Jolivette, Leone & Mathur, 2010). Altschuler et al. (2009) promote overarching case management (OCM) as a key strategy for transition, reentry, and aftercare. Two ways in which OCM promotes systems coordination are the development of a consolidated case plan and "service brokerage with community resources and linkage to non-correctional youth-serving agencies and groups" (Altschuler et al., 2009).

Create Opportunities for Success in Employment. Young adults leaving incarceration may have more difficulty obtaining employment both because of their correctional record and their lack of employment history. This makes it essential to offer career preparation opportunities – including life skills and soft skills training – during confinement, and employment support after release (Hagner, Malloy, Mazzone & Cormier, 2008; Harris, 2006). Community service, internships, paid work experience, and unsubsidized employment can be vehicles for learning employability for incarcerated youth (Harris, 2006). To facilitate post-release employment, Altschuler, Stangler, Berkley & Burton (2009) recommend that juvenile justice agencies create partnerships with local employers willing to interview ex-offenders and modify rules for group care settings to allow youth to build employment experience.

Consider the Use of Diversion and Graduated Sanctions to Prevent Youth from Entering the Juvenile Justice System. For youth committing minor offenses, diversion into community-based treatment and case management is a popular proposal as an alternative to confinement. However, this is a subject of debate. Some would make the argument that diversion should be the policy of choice because it avoids the negative consequences of imprisonment for the individual youth, and because reducing youth imprisonment rates overall means having more resources to treat those who undeniably need to receive treatment while being in confinement (Stenhjem 2005; Grisso, 2008). However, that policy may not be in the interest of the TAY offender. A study of the effectiveness of diversion (case management and residential services) concluded it was only minimally effective in preventing re-arrest among 18 to 25 year olds, whereas it was much more effective for older individuals (Hartwell, Fisher & Davis, 2007).

Behavioral Health

The literature showed the following recommendations for the behavioral health system in enhancing services for TAY with disabilities:
- Adopt Recovery-Oriented Systems of Care
- Assert State Leadership for Interagency Coordination
- Establish System Responsibility for Providing Services
- Align Eligibility in the Youth and Adult Service Systems
- Improve Availability of Services
- Provide Support for Navigating System Transition
- Promote the Use of Evidence-Based Approaches
- Train Service Providers to Specialize in Transition
- Increase State and Federal Attention to the Needs of TAY

Each of these recommendations and the cited literature are discussed in more detail below.

Adopt recovery-oriented systems of care. The concept of "systems of care" addresses many of the concerns about fragmentation and poor service coordination. Systems of care refer to "an organizational philosophy and framework that involves collaboration across agencies, families, and youth for the purpose of improving access and expanding the array of coordinated community-based, culturally and linguistically competent services and supports for children and youth with a serious emotional disturbance and their families" (Technical Assistance Partnership for Child and Family Mental Health, n.d.). Furthermore, the American Psychological Association (APA) recommends adopting recovery-oriented treatment as the dominant approach for mental health systems of care and support services for TAY (APA, n.d.).

Capturing the perspectives of both the addictions and mental health fields, participants at the 2005 Center for Substance Abuse Treatment National Summit on Recovery identified the 17 elements of recovery-oriented systems of care and services listed in Table 2.

Table 2. Elements of Recovery-Oriented Systems of Care

1. Person-centered
2. Inclusive of family and other ally involvement
3. Individualized and comprehensive services across the lifespan
4. Systems anchored in the community
5. Continuity of care
6. Partnership-consultant relationships
7. Strength-based
8. Culturally responsive
9. Responsiveness to personalo belief systems
10. Commitment to peer recovery support services
11. Inclusion of the voices and experiences of recovering individuals and their families
12. Integrated services
13. System-wide education and training
14. Ongoing monitoring and outreach
15. Outcomes driven
16. Research based
17. Adequately and flexibly financed

Source: Sheedy & Whitter, 2009

Researchers are beginning to explore the implementation and delivery of recovery-oriented services in the mental health system. The experiences of Philadelphia and Connecticut are two early examples. As Connecticut sought to establish recovery as the overarching philosophy of its publicly funded system of care, it adopted the following strategies over the course of several years:

1. Developing core values and principles based on the input of people in recovery;
2. Establishing a conceptual framework based on this vision of recovery;
3. Building workforce competencies and skills through training, education, and consultation;
4. Changing programs and service structures;
5. Aligning fiscal and administrative policies in support of recovery; and
6. Monitoring, evaluating, and adjusting the efforts (Sheedy & Whitter, 2009).

A 2005 statewide assessment of recovery-oriented practices agencies found that mental health professionals, persons in recovery, and family members in Connecticut "generally agreed that their agencies were providing services that are consistent with a recovery orientation" (O'Connell, Tondora, Croog, Evans, & Davidson in Sheedy & Whitter, 2009).

Assert state leadership for interagency coordination. Achieving continuity of care across relevant service agencies could be facilitated with state- or local-level interagency agreements, task forces, or coordination plans that address transition supports (Davis & Sondheimer, 2005; Davis, 2005; Woolsey & Katz-Leavy, 2008; GAO, 2008b). Other strategies for coordinating services across state agencies include establishing formal referral processes, and establishing integrated eligibility determination and service delivery (GAO, 2008b). States are also encouraged to improving services for TAY through targeted legislation and funding, and by more effectively utilizing Medicaid funding and service options (Woolsey & Katz-Leavy, 2008). Finally, states could engage in resource mapping and strategic planning to enhance cross-agency collaboration (Larson, 2009).

Establish system responsibility for providing transition services. Because transition services straddle the youth and adult mental health systems, either or both systems could be responsible for offering them (APA, n.d.; Davis, Geller & Hunt, 2006). Alternatively, one system could assume entire responsibility for providing transition services. The youth system could continue providing care for adolescents through age 25 or 30 to ensure continuity (Davis, n.d.), or the adult mental health system could prepare adolescents to transition into its system (APA, n.d.).

Align eligibility in the youth and adult service systems. Given that different definitions for mental health conditions in the child and adult systems are a cause for discontinuity of services, aligning definitions (and thus eligibility) across the two systems could help address the situation. Hoffman, Heflinger, Athay & Davis (2009) offer two distinct approaches for aligning definitions across the systems. One would be to extend the broader child system definition further into adulthood ("grandfathering") and the other would be aligning child and adult system definitions/policies on a condition-by-condition basis.

An approach to providing continuous service delivery across the transition period that bypasses service eligibility has been adopted in some very rare cases by what Davis (2007) refers to as "pioneering transition programs" – programs that serve youth continuously across the transition age. These programs have achieved "age flexibility" by combining streams of funding to provide services after youth would typically have left their program. The funding sources Davis identified that these programs were using included billable Medicaid hours, state or local mental health funds, private foundation grants, funds from other systems, and the like. For these programs, funding from the public mental health system came from either the child or adult mental health agency, but never both. She concluded that it was easier for this type of project to obtain funding when local decision makers have autonomy, and that "statewide funding initiatives that allow for the extension of programs across the transition age appear to be uncommon" (Davis, 2007).

Improve availability of developmentally-appropriate services. The current scarcity of services could be addressed by making sure that a variety of developmentally-appropriate services are offered at multiple locations, from which consumers, their families, and counselors could construct individualized service plans (APA, n.d.; Davis, 2005). This may require identifying and leveraging funding from all levels (Woolsey & Katz-Leavy, 2008). One model program profiled in the literature suggests that states could commission an assessment of system services gaps from a third party which can also provide technical assistance (Davis, Jivanjee & Koroloff, 2010). Beyond geographic availability, states need to make sure that programs have capacity to serve additional consumers, and that they are accessible and appropriate to the target population (Davis, Geller & Hunt, 2006). Furthermore, appropriate mental health services need to be paired with appropriate services in other domains such as housing, education, and workforce development. This is most successful when the partnerships are formalized such as through an Memorandum of Understanding (MOU) (Woolsey & Katz-Leavy, 2008).

Provide support for navigating system transition. Even with better alignment, transitioning between systems will involve some disruption and stress. TAY "need support in establishing appropriate adult services and the means to pay for these services, and in moving from a trusted provider to someone unknown" (Manteuffel, Stephens, Sondheimer & Fisher, 2008). To achieve this goal, the Transition to Independence Process (TIP) mental health recovery service delivery model promotes "ensuring a safety net of support by involving a young person's parents, family members, and other informal and formal key players" (National Collaborative on Workforce & Disability for Youth, 2009).

Promote the use of evidence-based approaches. SAMHSA is moving towards using evidence-based assessments, interventions, and treatments, which was an emphasis in the CMHI and Emerging Adults Initiatives (SAMHSA, 2013). The APA recommends increasing funding for research to establish evidence-based best practices for serving TAY, and technical assistance to help more programs adopt them (APA, n.d.). One example of an evidence-based approach is the Transition to Independence Process (TIP) model, central to which is the practice of "[tailoring] services and supports to be accessible, coordinated, appealing, non-stigmatizing, developmentally-appropriate, and build on strengths to enable the young people to pursue their goals across all transition domains" (Clark, 2009). Nevertheless, additional research and expertise is still needed in serving this age group and disability population (Davis, n.d.). Nonetheless, when practitioners encounter conditions and situations that do not benefit from clear evidence-based solutions, they can adopt a mindset of "evidence-based thinking" – selecting treatment based on a reasonable assessment that the approach will work and will be appropriate for the consumer (Morris, Day & Schoenwald, 2010).

Train service providers to specialize in transition. TAY are a population with a unique set of needs. There should be a professionally-trained service provider workforce to specialize in giving them the support they need (APA, n.d.). Specifically, there could be a subset of adult system case managers that are cross-trained to specialize in serving TAY (Davis & Sondheimer, 2005).

Increase state and Federal attention to the needs of TAY. The needs of TAY are receiving more focused attention on the Federal level because of three Federal interagency workgroups coordinating efforts to better serve TAY and others with disabilities including serious mental illnesses – the Federal Executive Steering Committee on Mental Health, the Shared Youth Vision Federal Collaborative Partnership, and the Federal Partners in Transition Workgroup (GAO, 2008b). But, according to researchers, there are areas for improvement. First, the Federal government could design and fund more pilot and demonstration projects to explore promising approaches (Woolsey & Katz-Leavy, 2008). In addition, it could conduct more research based on state-level Medicaid data as a policy tool to drive attention to this population and the performance of the publicly funded service systems (Heflinger & Hoffman, 2008). It could also provide more aid to states specifically for transition services, particularly those that "embrace person-centered planning or TIP-system planning processes that include the mental health system" (Hoffman, Heflinger, Athay & Davis, 2009). In their review of the efforts of child mental health systems to serve TAY, Davis and Sondheimer (2005) observed that the states that had made significant progress in improving transition services were those that had received funding to do so, rather than those who had attempted to shift resources from other services. In addition, on the state level, policymakers should prioritize collecting relevant data, creating task forces, and holding conferences to increase the visibility of the needs of TAY (Davis & Sondheimer, 2005).

Workforce Investment

The literature contained the following recommendations for the Workforce Investment system in enhancing services for TAY with disabilities:
- Promote Inclusive Employment and Access to Workforce Investment Services
- Better Engage American Job Centers
- Increase Supported Education and Employment to Build Skills
- Coordinate Services and Improve Navigability
- Engage Diverse (Low-Income, Minority, ESL) Youth
- Enhance Summer Employment
- Revisit Performance Measures and Build Data Systems

Each of these recommendations and the cited literature are discussed in more detail below.

Promote Inclusive Employment and Access to Workforce Investment Services. In a survey of 136 students with severe disabilities, one-third participated in summer paid or unpaid work, while one-third of working youth were in segregated work environments. This does not follow recent policy that people with disabilities should be in integrated employment. With two-thirds not working, this is a missed opportunity. Findings from the NLTS-2 revealed that youth with disabilities who had paid work experience in high school had more positive post-school work outcomes. Given this finding, Carter and colleagues recommend helping youth access community-based work experience while still in high school. Specifically, for policy, they recommend "examining the ways in which current policies such as the IDEA, the Carl Perkins Act, and the Rehabilitation Act support the development of work experiences in natural settings and how they can be augmented to do so in future reauthorizations or in the development of new policies is an essential next step increasing access for youth with severe disabilities" (Carter, Austin, & Trainor, 2012).

The APHSA calls for improved services via WIA for youth with disabilities by applying universal design principles, which are "framework for the design of environments, infrastructure, products, and communication practices, as well as the delivery of programs and services, to be usable by and accessible to the widest range of individuals" (APHSA, 2012). Also, focusing on disconnected youth as a whole, the National Youth Employment Council recommends that disconnected youth with specific barriers, such as a disability, should be eligible for WIA without regard to their income (Thakur, 2012). While income eligibility is a consideration in general for WIA Youth

Services, a youth with disabilities' income will be counted separately from their family; so therefore, essentially they are eligible to receive services.

Better Engage American Job Centers. American Job Centers can help in the transition process by providing services for youth and specifically, youth with disabilities on an as-needed basis. American Job Centers have the capacity to serve youth in transition, and the National Center on Workforce & Disability provides recommendations for how American Job Centers can be more involved. American Job Centers can actively seek to help youth navigate the transition process by working with local schools, finding out if the schools contract out services, contacting transition teams, contacting parent groups, examining interagency agreements, becoming involved in the Local Workforce Investment Board (LWIB) or Youth Council, and making additional contacts (National Center on Workforce & Disability, n.d.).

Increase Supported Education and Employment to Build Skills. The National Collaborative on Workforce and Disability for Youth recommends supported education and employment for youth with mental health needs. In addition, all youth need to participate in education programs to help promote skill-building and learning in school-based programs. Youth also need specific career preparation and work-based learning programs to plan for future employment. Peer-to-peer mentoring and promoting youth leadership can also help with supporting youth in moving towards employment (Podmostko, 2007).

Carter and Lundsford (2005) reviewed employment outcomes for individuals with emotional and behavioral disorders (EBD). In their review of secondary education programs, they found that skill building in social, vocational, academic, and self-determination is helpful in promoting employment. Important support areas identified include community linkages, work supports, family involvement, and student involvement (Carter & Lunsford, 2005). Family involvement can help promote positive school outcomes by helping to build strengths in youth, accessing employment information, and assisting in reaching additional supports (Podmostko, 2007). Lindsay (2011) analyzes characteristics and employment for youth with disabilities using the 2006 Participation and Activity Limitation Study. Findings show that youth who had disability for a long time were more likely to be employed than those recently diagnosed. Transportation is a factor in employment. Older youth (20-24) worked more hours per week or were more likely to be self-employed than younger youth (15-19). From the research, they recommend that rehabilitation and life skills transition teams pay special attention to those youth who may need extra support in reaching employment (Lindsay, 2011).

Brown and Thakur focused broadly on older youth and workforce development. Based on a review of the research, they developed "common operating principles" for helping all youth transition, which includes high quality standards-based education, preparatory experiences, work-based experiences, youth development and youth leadership, and connecting activities to support services (Brown & Thakur, 2006).

Youth need help navigating the plethora of programs available, connecting programs together, and accessing wraparound programs –such as mental and physical health services, transportation, tutoring, and financial planning (Fernandes & Gabe, 2009; Podmostko, 2007). Family involvement can also help provide supports for transitioning youth (Podmostko, 2007). The Next Generation: Youth Work Coalition recommended a policy to support youth workforce development using a Federal Youth Development Coordinating Council as a mechanism to do so. Authors called for expanding support that is currently available, removing legislative/administrative barriers to support youth workers, and allowing youth workers to become engaged in decision-making on government workforce programs (Cole & Ferrier, 2009). The APHSA also provided recommendations for promoting employment among people with disabilities, not specifically focused on youth, which included improved coordination among programs serving this population (Medicaid Infrastructure Grants, Real Choice Systems Change, Disability Employment Initiative) (APHSA, 2012).

Engage Diverse (Low-Income, Minority, ESL) Youth. Trainor and colleagues (2008) wrote a position paper, entitled *Opportunities for Diverse Youths with Disabilities: A Position Paper of the Division on Career Development* *and Transition*, and called for a need to better support diverse youth (such as low income, minority, and English as a second language) with disabilities through an ecological approach. The ecological approach considers multiple influences that impact youth and acknowledges "the complex sociocultural, political, and historical contexts in which transition education occurs." As such, larger social and system trends should be taken into account when planning interventions because such "macrosystemic realities," like poverty and unemployment, can prevent diverse youth with disabilities from accessing opportunities (Trainor et al., 2008).

Enhance Summer Employment. Summer employment may also be a way to help youth gain necessary work skills. Carter and colleagues recommend a multi-faceted approach using schools, families, and communities to increase the number of youth with disabilities accessing summer employment opportunities (Carter et al., 2010).

Revisit Performance Measures and Build Data Systems. In 2002, a study was conducted of how youth with disabilities were being served in the WIA system across six sites. A key recommendation was that sites needed help to develop "enhanced performance standards which measures progress in more refined gradations." This recommendation was for the USDOL to revisit the performance outcomes for numeracy and literacy. In addition to enhancing measures, other recommendations included the need to build a more effective data collection system to help sites collect more accurate data. One example cited at that time was that data was not collected on how many youth with disabilities were being served, the type of disability, and the services that youth with disabilities were accessing (Kaufman et al., 2005). At this time, however, USDOL collects information on how many youth with disabilities are being served as well as how many youth are getting each of the ten program elements. These ten program elements can be grouped around four major themes: 1) Improving Educational Achievement: tutoring, study skills training, dropout prevention strategies, and alternative secondary school services, 2) Preparing for and Succeeding in Employment: summer employment opportunities, paid and unpaid work experiences, and occupational skill training; 3) Providing Adequate Support in Completing Learning and Employment Goals: supportive services, adult mentoring, appropriate follow-up services, and comprehensive guidance and counseling; and 4) Developing the Potential of Youth as Citizens and Leadership: leadership development opportunities, which may include community service and peer-centered activities encouraging responsibility and other positive social behaviors during non-school hours.[11]

---

11 Information retrieved from Training and Employment Guidance Letter NO. 5-12 http://wdr.doleta.gov/directives/attach/TEGL/ TEGL_5_12_Acc.pdf.

VI. Common Themes

This section describes the common themes across each of the five systems. First, we outline findings from other systematic reviews of programs serving TAY. Then, we outline common trends across the systems.

Findings from Systematic Reviews

Overall, the evidence base on serving transition-aged youth, and especially youth with disabilities, has been limited. In 2010, Landmark and colleagues conducted a review of best practices in the transition process for youth receiving special education services from 29 articles from 1985 to 2009. Paid or unpaid work experience was the most substantiated best practice in the literature. Specifically, having a paid or unpaid job in high school was linked to successful employment and outcomes post-high school. Secondly, participation in an employment preparation program, including vocational and employment training, was seen to promote positive outcomes. Other research has shown that general education inclusion has promoted positive outcomes, meaning students with disabilities involved in general education curriculum. Family involvement in the transition process is also a best practice. Training in social skills, daily living, and self-determination have also all been measures of post-high school success for students with disabilities. Finally, the least empirically substantiated practice, was community and agency collaboration. Some literature did find that employment support agency support while youth were employed was helpful in promoting positive outcomes (Landmark, Ju, & Zhang, 2010).

Another systematic review from 2009 (Cobb & Alwell) analyzed 31 studies around transition planning for youth with disabilities. Their review showed that "student focused planning" and career planning around specific job skills helped with increasing positive outcomes. Three studies showed that where students were able to build their own transition plans, they had improved outcomes. Additionally, across studies, researchers noted a "perceived lack of efficacy of special education curricula." Vocational training also can help these youth by building work experience and promoting career development. Of the reviewed studies, many called for flexibility in providing tailored supports to this population (Cobb & Alwell, 2009).

Trends Across Systems in the Literature

Additional Research and Empirically-Validated Studies. For the most part, the research around TAY with disabilities is scarce. While there has been research on the TAY population as a whole, the specific population of TAY with disabilities is lacking. Cobb and Alwell (2009) note that there is a lack of studies on comprehensive transition models to understand what models are effective. Other researchers argue that "pilot projects and demonstration projects are needed to combine the 'best practice' factors together using applied research methods and appropriate outcome measures. More research is needed about models that work and outcomes that matter" (Stewart et al., 2010; see also Manteuffel, Stephens, Sondheimer & Fisher, 2008; Woolsey & Katz-Leavy, 2008). More information is needed on building customized employment models for individuals with disabilities (Elinson et al., 2010). Additionally, more rigorous evaluation is needed to understand the role of programs and services for TAY, particular for VR services (Honeycutt et al., 2013; NCD, 2008). In addition, more research is needed about what models work for specific subpopulations, such as females (Baltodano, Mathur & Rutherford, 2010), and what makes services appealing to TAY (Koroloff & Davis, 2010). Additional research providing data on this population has the ability to be utilized as a policy tool to drive attention to this population and the performance of the publicly funded service systems (Heflinger & Hoffman, 2008).

Eligibility and Access. Programs serving TAY vary in terms of eligibility requirements and age cutoffs. Of the systems discussed, there is inconsistency in the age limits for programs targeted toward TAY (GAO, 2008b; Koyanagi & Alfano, 2012). In fact, a 2005 national experts panel on youth transition policy voted as one of its top three policy priorities the following- "define this population clearly at the Federal level by emphasizing developmentally appropriate functioning to define disability, by using non-stigmatizing language, and by eliminating definitions and eligibility criteria that would exclude part of this age group by virtue of age" (Davis

& Koyanagi, 2005). In a simpler approach, some researchers suggest that eligibility criteria for transition-related programs should be increased to 24 or 25 (Bridgeland & Mason-Elder, 2012; Koyanagi & Alfano, 2012).

The APHSA also recommends timely reauthorization of the Work Incentives Planning and Assistance (WIPA) and Protection and Advocacy for Beneficiaries of Social Security (PABSS) programs to continue the promotion of work incentives; and to allow states to define their own age limits with Medicaid Buy-In programs to help promote employment among people with disabilities (APHSA, 2012).

The Federal government has begun to make a shift to serving older youth. Specifically, the Fostering Connections Act of 2008 changed eligibility requirements for youth in foster care from 18 to 21. Osgood and colleagues argue that this Act "marks a philosophical shift toward acknowledging continuing state responsibility to act *in loco parentis*[12] for foster youth into early adulthood" (Osgood et al., 2010).

In some cases, youth become too old and age out of being eligible for services as children, which requires a redetermination of benefits to be eligible as an adult (Medicaid and Social Security in particular) (Hemmeter et al., 2009; Hoffman, Heflinger, Athay & Davis, 2009). As youth age out of programs designed specifically for them, they enter programs that serve adults which may not be "equipped to address the special issues of young adulthood" (Osgood, Foster, & Courtney, 2010). These youth may also have difficulty accessing adult services (Moreno et al., 2013). Additionally, programs targeted for youth may not be successful in engaging older youth (Koyanagi & Alfano, 2012).

Regardless of eligibility and access challenges, there is a need to provide a "continuity of care" for youth from ages 14 or 16 to ages 25 or 30 across child and adult serving systems (Altschuler, 2005; Davis, n.d.; Davis & Sondheimer, 2005; Hoffman, Heflinger, Athay & Davis, 2009; Manteuffel, Stephens, Sondheimer & Fisher, 2008; Stewart, et al., 2010).

Additionally, eligibility for some programs might change as youth are able to secure gainful employment. This has been specifically cited for Social Security, but it is a consideration for all systems (Green et al., 2005; O'Leary et al., 2011). Simplified benefit programs and work incentives could encourage work and lessen fears of benefit loss (O'Day, 2012).

Increasing participation in programs is also a consideration for all systems. The literature cites that participation in education and employment support programs is low among TAY with disabilities (Carter et al., 2010; Grigal, Hart, Migiliore, 2011). Increasing participation depends on a number of factors, including providers' service capacity, the age-appropriateness of the program, accessibility, and whether or not the services are appealing (Davis, Geller, & Hunt, 2006). A GAO report on services connecting disconnected youth to education and employment found that over half of program directors said mental health services were insufficient or lacking in their communities (GAO, 2008a). More specifically, referral and identification is needed for youth while they are still in school, which requires local education agency (LEA) staff to bring VR personnel on board with transition planning (The Study Group, 2007).

Services designed to support TAY with disabilities may be inadequate. Specifically, Davis (2010) argues that youth with dual disabilities may be served inappropriately because the services they receive address only their developmental disability or their mental health condition, not both. To enhance youth services for those with co-occurring disorders, Hoffman and colleagues (2009) suggests a Federal policy for special education students with funding from CMHS/SAMHSA to provide resources for frequent, person-centered transition planning. A 2005 national experts panel on youth transition policy listed as its top priority for TAY-serving systems to "develop more transition support services and rapidly build interagency systems that offer comprehensive, coordinated, age-appropriate, youth-driven services" (Davis & Koyanagi, 2005). Dr. Maryann Davis, a researcher with the Center

---

12 Loco parentis is Latin for "in the place of a parent," and refers to the legal doctrine under which an individual assumes parental rights, duties, and obligations without going through the formalities of legal adoption.

for Mental Health Services Research at the University of Massachusetts Medical School makes the observation that policy should "[promote] a density of developmentally-appropriate services from which individualized service and treatment plans can be constructed" (Davis, n.d.).

Collaboration and Coordination. Collaboration across systems serving TAY with disabilities is an identified need in the literature. There is overlap among the systems that are serving these youth; for example, 35 percent of youth with emotional mental health disorders who are in special education are arrested as juveniles (Osgood et al., 2010). While agencies in each system address youth transition, their approach is often limited to their own sphere of expertise and outcome goals. For example, educators focus on success in post-secondary education and training while mental health care providers focus on skills needed to live independently, and so on. Federal laws that are perceived to limit the exchange of information among service providers further reinforce this segregation of services (Office of Disability Employment Policy, 2013).

Researchers have argued that there is misalignment across programs serving TAY, but also that there is not enough capacity and funding available for organizations to collaborate on transition planning (Hoffman, Heflinger, Athay & Davis, 2009; Koyanagi & Alfano, 2012). Specifically, there is not enough capacity among organizations to work collaboratively, and there is an "absence of an overarching framework for systems and service integration" (Koyanagi & Alfano, 2012). Additionally, VR agencies need additional funding to be a part of the transition process from the time youth are still in school, and LEAs and VR agencies should build agreements and integrated data systems to align service delivery (The Study Group, 2007).

Not only is there a lack of coordination between youth-serving systems, but also between child- and adult-serving systems (Heflinger & Hoffman, 2008; Koyanagi & Alfano, 2012; Osgood et al., 2010). There is a need for systemic integration, particularly for mental health and juvenile justice systems (Hoffman, Heflinger, Athay & Davis, 2009). Researchers have raised concerns with having a fragmented service delivery system where each agency has its own "individual eligibility criteria, case plans, records, and there is a lack of support to communicate or coordinate with other agencies" (Stenhjem, 2005). In a study of state policies, only a minority reported having interagency agreements and/or committees that could facilitate transition supports (Davis & Sondheimer, 2005).

Translation of this universal recommendation of coordination and collaboration into sound policy remains an elusive topic in the literature. There are examples of individual school systems, workforce development agencies, and adult service providers coming together to integrate services, but they appear to be motivated by special initiative funding (such as YTD) or individual initiative (for example, see Brown, Brown & Glaser, 2013).

As previously discussed, the Youth Transition Funders Group argues for collaboration between schools and employment agencies to help promote work experience as well as keep students in school moving toward a diploma. They argue that the way to do this is to hold the school systems accountable and "revisit statewide information systems to produce analytics providing timely feedback to mayors, superintendents and state managers on the well-being of our youth" (Sturgis, 2013).

In case studies of promising transition programs for youth with mental health needs, programs with the most successful partnerships have formalized the relationship, such as through a Memorandum of Understanding (MOU) (Woolsey & Katz-Leavy, 2008). The GAO specifically highlighted successful strategies for state agency collaboration, including formal referral processes across agencies and integrated eligibility determination (GAO, 2008b).

The Transition Service Integration Model is one example of a framework for how multiple service systems could integrate resources and expertise (Hoffman, Heflinger, Athay & Davis, 2009). In this model, providers from the vocational rehabilitation, post-secondary education, American Job Centers, Social Security, mental health, and other systems are resources for a youth's Local Project Management Team. Work-based experience, especially paid employment, is seen as a key component, since work experience is the strongest predictor of post-school employment success (Luecking, 2008). This model has been further developed and is being tested as the Maryland Seamless Transition Collaborative; it has also been cross-walked with the National Collaborative on Workforce and Disability for Youth's *Guideposts for Success*. Early findings of the evaluation indicate that 63 percent of students receiving services organized within the framework had "achieved the optimum seamless transition; that is, they were employed in individualized, inclusive jobs (26 percent), enrolled in postsecondary education (23 percent), or employed and enrolled in postsecondary education (14 percent)" (Luecking & Luecking, 2013).

Promote a Single National Collaborative Policy. Researchers who have analyzed policies around vulnerable youth have also a suggested developing a single national policy focused on youth in transition as a lack of coordination across national, state, and local levels for serving transition-age youth has been cited (Fernandes, 2012; Moreno, Honeycutt, McLeod, & Gill, 2013). Such a policy/strategy could begin to align Federal policy serving this population. Recent work has suggested aligning IDEA and the Rehabilitation Act with the Higher Education Opportunities Act, and adding provisions to increase access to employment and postsecondary education (Grigal et al., 2011). Others have similarly called for serving this population within a single, integrated system rather than from a multitude of independent systems (Osgood et al., 2011).

Other countries have been successful in serving youth in transition by mandating that employers hire people with disabilities, using vouchers to help individuals access vocational rehabilitation training programs, and increasing coordination across government levels (Moreno, Honeycutt, McLeod, & Gill, 2013). State policy can also be amended to incorporate the range of services, incorporating the "health, vocational, educational, residential, financial, and legal service systems as collaborative partners" (Pottick et al., 2008).

However, in recent years there have been Federal efforts to improve coordination for programs serving youth - although as Fernandes (2012) notes only one of such plans has been funded: the YouthBuild Transfer Act. The Act transferred the YouthBuild program from the U.S. Department of Housing and Urban Development to the U.S. Department of Labor due to its focus on workforce and training. Additionally, in 2008, President Bush established an Interagency Working Group on Youth Programs through an Executive Order. In 2009, the Working Group was tasked with holding meetings around the country to ultimately develop a strategic plan for youth programming. As of 2012, the Working Group had put together a framework to guide the plan's development, focused on the following three outcomes: "health, safety, and wellness; school, family, and community engagement and connections; and education, training, employment, transitions, and readiness for careers and adulthood" (Fernandes, 2012). Most recently, the Office of Planning, Research and Evaluation within the Administration for Children and Families within the U.S. Department of Health and Human Services released a Framework for Advancing the Well-Being and Self-Sufficiency of At-Risk Youth, built on the theories of risk and resilience and capital development. While this framework addresses the broader population of at-risk youth, it echoes recommendations listed here for programming specific to youth with disabilities, such as youth engagement in service planning, strengthening families when appropriate, and increasing human capital by providing evidence-informed services to prepare youth for economic self-sufficiency (Dion et al., 2013).

Additionally, some states have begun to integrate data systems to promote streamlined data collection and reduce duplication of effort for legislative requirements, as the IDEA and Elementary and Secondary Education Act have overlapping reporting requirements. State school systems have been developing comprehensive, longitudinal data systems to track students with disabilities from K-12 through postsecondary activities. Such integrated data systems align with the Obama's administration's educational reform and Data Quality Campaign (Muller, 2010).

Coordinated, Focused Planning and Accountability. Coordinated planning is also a way to help youth build the necessary support system to be successful once transitioned into employment (O'Leary et al., 2011). Walters and colleagues (2011) argue that the research supports the recommendation that transition planning for foster care youth should focus on permanency as the end goal (Walters et al., 2011). Such transition plans should be built from a comprehensive strength-based assessment that identifies the youth's skills and developmental level, and identifies goals and future objectives (Hagner, Malloy, Mazzone & Cormier, 2008; Podmostko, 2007; Walters, et al.

2011). The services provided should be "flexible, supportive, and customizable to individual needs" (Manteuffel, Stephens, Sondheimer & Fisher, 2008). Youth should be involved in transition planning conversations, and in some cases, they can lead the transition planning meeting. All agencies involved in the lives of the youth should be included in the transition planning. Agencies should be engaged in continuous quality improvement of their transition efforts (Gonsoulin, Darwin & Read, 2012). Finally, a consideration for collaboration and coordination is developing accountability - both across systems as well as within systems between children and adult services - to help youth meet their goals, and data sharing agreements with consideration for privacy rights of the population served (Bridgeland & Mason-Elder, 2012; Chaplin, O'Hara, Holt & Bouras, 2009; Koyanagi & Alfano, 2012; Walters et al., 2009).

Luecking and Luecking (2013) provide a descriptive overview of the Maryland Seamless Transition Collaborative (MSTC), which was funded through the U.S. Department of Education, Rehabilitation Services Administration. The Collaborative was charged with designing a model of transition services. Eligible youth who are "presumed eligible" for state VR services receive services in 10th grade or three years prior to exiting secondary school. The model is built on active participation of a VR counselor in transition planning. Early outcomes show that 63 percent of students at the point of transition had been employed, enrolled in postsecondary education, or both. The model is built on the NCWD/Y's *Guideposts for Success*, which includes the components of:
- Discovery: an assessment of student strengths, needs, interests, and goals.
- Individualized Work-Based Experiences: interviews, job-site tours, unpaid or paid internships.
- Individualized Paid Inclusive Employment: student is hired by an employer and primarily works with people who do not have disabilities.
- Family supports: involvement with families through each activity, including discovery, job planning, and training in how to manage benefits (like SSI or SSDI).
- Early VR agency case initiation: VR actively participates in transition plan and to develop an IEP with the student and family.
- System linkages and collaboration: team structure to foster collaboration across agencies serving this population.
- Coordination with teachers and instructional staff: maintain relationships with education teachers, and transition team to collaborate with educational personnel.

Ensure Staff Training and Professional Development for Service Providers. Researchers have cited that many professionals serving TAY with disabilities need additional training in the developmental issues facing this population and to build expertise in serving this population (Balcazar et al., 2013; Grigal et al., 2011; Hoffman, Heflinger, Athay & Davis, 2009; Leone & Weinberg, 2010; Osgood, et al., 2011; Plotner, Trach, & Strauser, 2012; Stewart et al., 2010; The Study Group, 2007; Woolsey & Katz-Leavy, 2008). Few youth workforce agencies require staff training (Cole & Ferrier, 2009). Broadly, the American Psychological Association recommends developing a professionally trained mental and behavioral health workforce that can meet the needs of children, transition youth, and adults with severe mental illness (APA, n.d.). While there is a need to build education at all levels including youth, families, community members, service providers, and society on TAY programming (Stewart et al., 2010), some researchers offer the specific solution of cross-training a subset of adult system case managers to specialize in serving transition-age young adults (Davis & Sondheimer, 2005).

Professional development credentialing for service professionals preparing youth for the transition to adulthood is the focus of the National Collaborative on Workforce & Disability for Youth's recent Youth Service Professionals' Knowledge, Skills, and Abilities (YSP/KSAs) initiative. Research suggest that establishing a career pathway and professional development system would result in professionals having more comprehensive competencies across the fields of workforce development, youth development, education, counseling, and disability services. Crucial steps they identified for establishing such a system include developing joint commitment across youth-serving sectors, engaging Federal agencies, aligning the YSP/KSAs competencies with those of other youth-serving professional associations, building upon the existing credentialing opportunities, and increasing relevant pre-service coursework at institutions of higher education (National Collaborative on Workforce & Disability for Youth, 2012).

Tailor Transition Services for Culturally and Linguistically Diverse (CLD) Youth. TAY with disabilities accessing services from the five Federal systems studied span different cultures, races, and ethnicities, and may not use English as their first language. Some challenges reported by Latino youth and families in particular are:

- Language issues: There may be a lack of translation and interpretation services available for students and their families.
- Documentation of citizenship: Not having documentation can restrict individuals from receiving services from some systems. For example, a Social Security number is required to apply for VR services. Additionally, service providers may have trouble collaborating with undocumented parents who avoid contact with public officials.
- Culturally biased services: Transition service models may make inappropriate assumptions about goals and values. For example, providers may assume all TAY share the goal of moving out of their family's home and living independently after graduating from high school, while that may not be an expectation in some families.
- Family participation: Engaging parents can be challenging when they do not understand the goals of transition services, their role, whom they can go to with questions, or when limited language or education prevents them from feeling like part of the process.
- Lack of resources: There are many points in the transition planning process where additional resources would be helpful for assisting CLD youth: for more assistants in the classroom, for coordinating more culturally and linguistically appropriate work experience placements, and for more extracurricular opportunities (Povenmire-Kirk, Lindstrom, & Bullis, 2010).

Because of challenges like these and other structural barriers impeding their postsecondary success, it is all the more necessary to use person-centered planning with youth from historically marginalized groups[13] (Trainor, 2010).

Help Youth Navigate Services. Across all systems, youth and their families need supports to help them navigate services available (Heflinger & Hoffman, 2008; Podmostko, 2007; Stewart et al., 2010). In a qualitative study of youth involved in YTD, one-on-one relationships with counselors were vital to maintaining youth's drive to find work and to navigate the system. A possible recommendation to help youth access services from this research was also to have a liaison between the youth and service providers who could help youth obtain funding for higher education or vocational training. Long-term counseling might also help youth retain jobs or seek higher-level employment and may provide a sounding board for youth (O'Day, 2012). Difficulty navigating services across systems is not the only problem. Navigating and maximizing services within systems is difficult as well. Larson (2009) argues that the services provided through the WIA system "are largely self-directed and lack intensity, accommodations are not provided unless young people self-disclose their disability, and stringent performance measures discourage workforce service providers from serving individuals who need more intensive and longer term support" (Larson, 2009).

Conclusion

In conclusion, while the literature cited multiple challenges and barriers to serving TAY with disabilities across the Vocational Rehabilitation, Social Security, Juvenile Justice, Behavioral Health, and Workforce Investment Systems, it also provides comprehensive, detailed recommendations – many of which span across the five systems. TAY with disabilities represent an important population to engage in multiple services to help them build the capacity for long-term self-sufficiency.

---

13 According to the author, "Historical marginalization refers to bias, prejudice, and discrimination that groups have experienced over time because of institutional and individual racism, ethnocentrism, sexism, classism, and ableism" (Trainor, 2010).

VII. Appendix A. Authorizing Legislation

System	Authorizing Legislation
Vocational Rehabilitation	The Rehabilitation Act of 1973 authorizes the formula grant programs of vocational rehabilitation, supported employment, independent living, and client assistance. It also authorizes training and service discretionary grants administered by the Rehabilitation Services Administration (U.S. Department of Education, 2013). States match 21.3 percent of Federal funding received (U.S. Department of Education, 2013). Priority for vocational rehabilitation is given to participants with the most severe disabilities, and those eligible for SSI are presumed eligible. VR agencies provide services, which include comprehensive assessment, counseling, vocational training, transportation, transitional services, and supported employment services (Koyanagi & Alfano, 2012).
Social Security	Social Security was established in 1935 to provide retirement benefits for older adults (Guzman, Pirog, & Seefeldt, 2013). Later iterations of the law added Social Security Disability Insurance (1954 as Title II) and Supplemental Security Income (1974 as Title XVI). The programs provide income support and health benefits for youth (and adults) with disabilities (National Collaborative on Workforce & Disability for Youth, 2013). The Social Security Act defines disability strictly and includes complex eligibility requirements (Green, Eigen, Lefko, & Ebling, 2005). Recently, the SSA made a policy change to allow youth with disabilities transitioning out of foster care to apply for SSI benefits 90 days prior to their eighteenth birthday, as opposed to 30 days. This change was designed to reduce the potential for a gap in benefits for these youth (King & Rukh-Kamaa, 2013). The Ticket to Work and Work Incentives Improvement Act of 1999 - Public Law 106-170 authorized the Ticket to Work Program. An individual must be over the age of 18, receiving Social Security Disability Insurance (SSDI) or Supplemental Security Income (SSI), must have a disability for which medical improvement is not expected or possible; and the individual must live in a state where Tickets are available (National Collaborative on Workforce & Disability for Youth, 2013). The law was designed to give individuals with disabilities flexibility and choices in receiving employment support services, and addressed criticism that SSDI and SSI beneficiaries have disincentives to find work – in 1999, less than .05 percent of beneficiaries returned to work (Green et al., 2005). The Youth in Transition Demonstration was authorized by sections 234 and 1110 of the Social Security Act of 1935, which was amended in 1980 by Public Law 96-265. The amendments authorized demonstration projects to help beneficiaries return to work and the ability to waive rules around eligibility and benefit levels for beneficiaries that return to work (Martinez et al., 2010).

System	Authorizing Legislation
Juvenile Justice	Federal support for state-run juvenile justice facilities and programs is authorized by the Juvenile Justice and Delinquency Prevention Act (JJDPA) of 1974, P.L. 93-415. Two of the grant programs it authorizes are the Juvenile Justice and Delinquency Prevention State Formula Grants and the Title V Community Prevention Incentive Grants. The legislation has four areas of compliance for states: • Offenders whose crimes would not be punishable by imprisonment if they were adults (e.g., truancy) shall not be institutionalized; • Youth shall not be held in correctional facilities with adults; • Youth shall be separated from adult prisoners; and • States shall work to address the disproportionate imprisonment of minority offenders. JJDPA was reauthorized with the 21st Century Department of Justice Appropriations Authorization Act of 2002 (P.L. 107-273). Most significantly, it established the Juvenile Accountability Block Grants (JABG) program which codified the shift of the juvenile justice system from rehabilitation to accountability (Nuñez-Neto, 2007). The Safe Schools / Healthy Students program is authorized by three pieces of legislation: the Safe and Drug-Free Schools and Communities Act, 20 U.S.C. § 7131; the Public Health Services Act, 42 U.S.C. § 290aa; and the Juvenile Justice and Delinquency Prevention Act, 42 U.S.C. § 5614(b) (4) (e) and § 5781 et seq. (Koyanagi, 2012). Application of the Individuals with Disabilities Education Act of 2004 for this population was previously described in the section on Education/Vocational Rehabilitation. The No Child Left Behind (NCLB) Act is the 2004 reauthorization of the Elementary and Secondary Education Act. Title I, Part D, Subpart 1, Section 1418 addresses transition services for neglected, delinquent, or at-risk youth (U.S. Department of Education, 2006).
Mental Health	The Center for Mental Health Services at the Substance Abuse and Mental Health Services Administration (SAMHSA) awards Mental Health Block Grants (MHBG) to states. Funding was first awarded to states for mental health services with the passage of the Community Mental Health Centers Act in 1963. Like many other social programs, funding for mental health was shifted to block grant format, with the Omnibus Budget Reconciliation Act of 1981. The 1992 Alcohol, Drug Abuse, and Mental Health Administration (ADAMHA) Reorganization Act transferred this authority to SAMHSA (Gelman & Green, 2010; National Institute of Mental Health, 2013). Medicaid and the Children's Health Insurance Program are authorized on the Federal level by the Social Security Act, specifically Titles XIX and XXI. The Affordable Care Act (ACA) of 2010 allows states to expand their Medicaid programs to cover more qualifying children. In addition, the ACA made changes to Medicaid's 1915(i) program in the areas of expanding eligibility and eligibility protections, giving states flexibility to create new Medicaid categories to reach new populations, offering new services and target services to particular groups, and reducing states' ability to limit program availability (FamiliesUSA, n.d.; Klees, Wolfe & Curtis, 2011). The Substance Abuse Prevention and Treatment Block Grant has its roots in the Omnibus Budget Reconciliation Act of 1981, which established the Alcohol, Drug Abuse and Mental Health Services (ADMS) Block Grant. This grant was divided into two separate streams, one for mental health services and one for substance abuse services, by the ADAMHA Reorganization Act of 1992. Comprehensive Community Mental Health Services for Children and Their Families Program (also called the Children's Mental Health Initiative, or CMHI) is authorized by the 1992 ADAMHA Reorganization Act (Center for Mental Health Services, 2010).

System	Authorizing Legislation
Workforce Investment	The Workforce Investment Act (WIA) of 1998 (Public Law 105-220) is charged with authorizing Federal employment and training, adult education/literacy, and vocational rehabilitation for adults, disadvantaged youth, and dislocated workers. Specifically, the Act authorizes American Job Centers to provide streamlined service delivery and includes a non-discrimination clause (Center for Law and Social Policy, 2013; National Collaborative on Workforce & Disability for Youth, 2013). The Workforce Investment Act "mandates the creation of coordinated, effective, and customer-focused workforce development and employment services" (Brown & Thakur, 2006, p.92). The WIA includes provisions for youth to require states to help prepare youth for the workforce (Brown & Thakur, 2006). It is anticipated that WIA will be reauthorized in the coming months. The Center for Law and Social Policy provided recommendations for WIA reauthorization arguing that WIA should continue to include a youth funding line, which should require that half of those served should be high-risk, such as disabled youth (Harris & Bird, 2012). Also in relation to youth, the Center on Law and Social Policy (CLASP) recommends aligning Title 1 and II of the WIA within a career pathways framework. This would help integrate employment with adult education. Such an alignment would help youth access the training they need to achieve gainful employment or higher education (Ganzglass, 2010). Title 1, B of the Act authorizes formula grants and Title IV, Subtitle D authorizes nationally managed programs, includes a Youth Service Program. The program serves youth 14 to 21 who are low income and one or more of the following: deficient in basic literacy skills; a high school dropout; homeless; a runaway; or a foster child; pregnant or a parent; an offender; an individual who requires additional assistance to complete an educational program, or to secure and hold employment. Title 1, C includes residentially-based education and training programs and Job Corps, which has the same income and eligibility requirements as the Youth Service Programs but ages range from 16-24 and there is no upper age limit for an otherwise eligible individual with a disability (National Collaborative on Workforce & Disability for Youth, 2013). The youth program consists of the ten program elements required at WIA section 129(c), which include: tutoring, alternative secondary school offerings, summer employment opportunities, paid and unpaid work experience, occupational skill training, leadership development opportunities, supportive services, mentoring, follow-up services, and comprehensive guidance and counseling (Wagner et al., 2007).

VIII. Appendix B. Methodology

The U.S. Department of Labor Office of Disability Employment Policy commissioned a literature review to better understand the extent to which and how transition aged youth with disabilities are being served within five Federal systems (Mental Health, Social Security, Vocational Rehabilitation, Juvenile Justice, and Workforce Investment), and to identify recommendations that have been made to improve service delivery to youth with disabilities within these five systems over the past eight years. This appendix aims to summarize common and important points that appear in secondary research on the topic, from sources such as peer-reviewed journals, public agencies, policy researchers, and technical assistance providers.

This literature review addresses the following research questions:
1) What role does each system play in youth transition?
2) To what extent (e.g., number of youth served, number of youth estimated to be eligible for services, etc.), are youth with disabilities being served by each of these systems?
3) What legislation authorizes the program(s)?
4) What are the central programs and services for youth with disabilities provided by each system?
5) According to the literature, what are the challenges and barriers to serving youth with disabilities in the systems?
6) According to the literature, what are the recommendations (both state and Federal) for enhancing systems' capacity to serve youth with disabilities?
7) According to the literature, what are common themes or trends around transition both within and across systems?

The research team employed a systematic process for evaluating and reviewing resources for inclusion in the literature review. Our research collection involved four approaches:
- review of client-provided materials;
- search of databases for academic scholarly published sources;
- expansive search through reputable sources (e.g. think tanks and research institutes); and
- consultation with subject matter experts.

We started by reviewing approximately 50 materials provided by ODEP on transition services within and across the five systems, to build a strong foundation in the issues in serving this population. From there, we expanded our search to capture any more recent (2005 to present) research from academic scholarly published sources. We primarily used the EBSCOhost[14] electronic research solution, focusing on the databases represented in Table C-1: Research Databases in EBSCOhost, in addition to Google Scholar.

Table C-1. Research Databases in EBSCOhost

- Academic Search Complete
- Child Development & Adolescent Studies
- EconLit
- Education Research Complete
- Family & Society Studies Worldwide
- Family Studies Abstracts
- Health Policy Reference CenterProfessional Development Collection
- PsycARTICLES
- PsycBOOKS
- PsycEXTRA
- PsycINFO

---

14 EBSCO Information Services provides a complete and optimized research solution comprised of research databases, e-books, and e-journals to support the information and collection development needs of libraries and other institutions and to maximize the search experience for researchers and other end users.

- Psychology and Behavioral Science Collections
- Social Sciences Full Text
- Social Work Abstracts
- SocINDEX with Full Text

The key words we used for searching the databases included:
- Youth (and variations including adolescents, young adults)
- Disabilities (and variations including learning disabilities, physical disabilities, mental health, special needs)
- Transition (and variations including adulthood, emerging adults)
- System names:
  o Mental Health
  o Social Security
  o Vocational Rehabilitation
  o Juvenile Justice
  o Workforce Investment
  o Post-secondary Education
  o Cross-System collaboration (and variations including system-level, system coordination)

We used additional criteria for determining the relevancy of research for review. First, because the focus of the literature review was on the capacity of the five systems, we focused on research about systems-level outcomes and issues, rather than strictly individual-level outcomes. Second, because the systems in question are Federal, we looked at their programs, issues, and recommendations for improvement at the Federal level. For the systems that are strongly centralized in administration, such as Social Security, this meant that it was relatively straightforward to collect information on universal, Federal-level issues. For other systems that are more decentralized with services delivered by states, counties, and cities, such as the Juvenile Justice, Mental Health, Vocational Rehabilitation, and Workforce Investment systems, the programs, issues, and recommendations vary by jurisdiction. This preliminary literature review, then, sought to collect information on the mechanisms by which the Federal systems fund and support service delivery to the target population at the state and local levels, and the issues and recommendations for improving those mechanisms.

From this type of keyword search, we expanded our pool of articles by reviewing pertinent documents cited in the research we had identified. This also included identifying authors who were subject matter experts in their fields and looking for their recent relevant publications. Next, we searched for resources on the websites of relevant government agencies, such as the Social Security Administration, the Office of Juvenile Justice and Delinquency Prevention, and the Department of Education. Then, we searched for research and policy papers from non-public, non-academic organizations that commonly receive Federal funding to do research on this population or these systems, such as National Collaborative on Workforce and Disability for Youth (NCWD/Youth), the Bazelon Center for Mental Health Law, and the Center for Law and Social Policy (CLASP). Finally, we consulted with subject matter experts in the fields of Mental Health, Juvenile Justice, and Social Security who identified additional resources, which we incorporated.

IX. References

Altschuler, D.M. (2005). Policy and Program Perspectives on the Transition to Adulthood for Adolescents in the Juvenile Justice System. In D.W. Osgood, E.M. Foster, C. Flanagan, & G.R. Ruth (Eds.) *On Your Own Without a Net: The Transition to Adulthood for Vulnerable Populations* (pp. 92-113). Chicago: University of Chicago Press.

Altschuler, D., Stangler, G., Berkley, K., & Burton, L. (2009). *Supporting Youth in Transition to Adulthood: Lessons Learned from Child Welfare and Juvenile Justice.* Washington, DC: Center for Juvenile Justice Reform.

American Psychological Association. (n.d.) *Transition Youth with Serious Mental Illness.*

APHSA. (2012). Employment for People with Disabilities: A Pathways policy brief. Washington, DC: APHSA. Retrieved from http://www.aphsa.org/content/dam/CWD/PDF/Home/Disabilities-Policy-Brief.pdf.

Balcazar, F.E., Oberoi, A., & Keel, J.M. (2013). *Predictors of Employment and College Attendance Outcomes for Youth in Transition: Implications for Policy and Practice.* Journal of Applied Rehabilitation Counseling 44(1), 38-45.

Baltodano, H. M., Mathur, S. R., & Rutherford, R. B. (2005). *Transition of Incarcerated Youth with Disabilities Across Systems and into Adulthood.* Exceptionality, 13(2), 103-124. doi:10.1207/s15327035ex1302_4.

Bazelon Center for Mental Health Law. (2008a). *Moving On: Federal Programs to Assist Transition-Age Youth with Serious Mental Health Conditions: Health Services.*

Bazelon Center for Mental Health Law. (2008b). *Moving On: Federal Programs to Assist Transition-Age Youth with Serious Mental Health Conditions: Mental Health Programs.*

Bazelon Center for Mental Health Law. (2008c). *Moving On: Federal Programs to Assist Transition-Age Youth with Serious Mental Health Conditions: Substance Abuse Programs.*

Bazelon Center for Mental Health Law. (2008d). *Moving On: Federal Programs to Assist Transition-Age Youth with Serious Mental Health Conditions: Youth Involved with or at Risk of Involvement in Juvenile Justice.*

Bazelon Center for Mental Health Law. (2011). *Funding for Mental Health Services and Programs.*

Belfield, C. R., Levin, H. M., & Rosen, R. (2012). *The Economic Value of Opportunity Youth.* Washington, DC: Civic Enterprises. Retrieved from http://www.civicenterprises.net/MediaLibrary/Docs/econ_value_opportunity_youth.pdf.

Ben-Shalom, Y. & Stapleton, D. (2013). *Trends in the Composition and Outcomes of Young Social Security Disability Awardees."* Michigan Retirement Research Center (MRRC) Working Paper, WP 2013-284. Retrieved from http://www.mrrc.isr.umich.edu/publications/papers/pdf/wp284.pdf.

Ben-Shalom, Y., Stapleton, D., Phelps, D., & Bardos, M. (2012). *Longitudinal statistics for new Supplemental Security Income beneficiaries.* Washington, DC: Mathematica Policy Research.

Bloom, D., Thompson, S. L., & Ivry, R. (2010). *Building a Learning Agenda Around Disconnected Youth.* New York, NY: MDRC.

Bridgeland, J., & Mason-Elder, T. (2012). *A Bridge to Reconnection.* Washington, DC: Civic Enterprises.

Brown, L., Brown, S., & Glaser, S. (2013). Improved Transition Outcomes for Students with Visual Impairments Through Interagency Collaboration. *Journal of Visual Impairment & Blindness, 107(6),* 406–408.

Brown, D. E., & Thakur, M. B. (2006). Workforce Development for Older Youth. N*ew Directions for Youth Development (111),* 91-104.

Burdette, P. (2008). Graduation Requirements for Students with Disabilities: Policy Recommendations. *Project Forum.* Alexandria, VA: National Association of State Directors of Special Education.

Camacho, C. B., & Hemmeter, J. (2012). Linking Youth Transition Support Services: Results from Two Demonstration Projects. *Social Security Bulletin, 73*(1), 59-71.

Carney, K.J. (n.d.) *EDJJ Professional Development Series Module 2: Characteristics of Incarcerated Youth with Disabilities.* College Park, MD: The National Center on Education, Disability, and Juvenile Justice.

Carter, E. W., Austin, D., & Trainor, A. A. (2012). Predictors of Postschool Employment Outcomes for Young Adults with Severe Disabilities. *Journal of Disability Policy Studies, 23*(1), 50-63.

Carter, E. W., Ditchman, N., Sun, Y., Trainor, A. A., Swedeen, B., & Owens, L. (2010). Summer Employment and Community Experiences of Transition-age Youth with Severe Disabilities. *Exceptional Children, 76*(2), 194-212.

Carter, E. W., & Lunsford, L. B. (2005). Meaningful work: Improving Employment Outcomes for Transition-age Youth with Emotional and Behavioral Disorders. *Preventing School Failure, 49*(2), 63-69.

Cavanaugh, D., Goldman, S., Friesen, B., Bender, C., & Le, L. (2009). *Designing a Recovery-Oriented Care Model for Adolescents and Transition Age Youth with Substance Use or Co-occurring Mental Health Disorders.* Rockville, MD: Substance Abuse and Mental Health Services Administration, Center for Substance Abuse Treatment and Center for Mental Health Services.

Center for Behavioral Health Statistics and Quality, Substance Abuse and Mental Health Services Administration. (2012). *National Survey on Drug Use and Health.* Retrieved from http://www.samhsa.gov/data/NSDUH/2k11MH_FindingsandDetTables/2K11MHFR/NSDUHmhfr2011.htm.

Center for Mental Health Services, Substance Abuse and Mental Health Services Administration, U.S. Department of Health and Human Services. (2010). *The Comprehensive Community Mental Health Services for Children and Their Families Program, Evaluation findings—Annual Report to Congress, 2010* (PEP12-CMHI2010). Retrieved from http://store.samhsa.gov/shin/content/PEP12-CMHI2010CD/PEP12-CMHI2010CD.pdf.

Chaplin, E., O'Hara, J., Holt, G., & Bouras, N. (2009). Mental Health Services for People with Intellectual Disability: Challenges to Care Delivery. *British Journal of Learning Disabilities, 37*(2), 157-164.

Cheatham, G. A., Smith, S. J., Elliott, W., & Friedline, T. (2013). Family Assets, Postsecondary Education, and Students with Disabilities: Building on Progress and Overcoming Challenges. *Children and Youth Services Review 35*(7): 1078–1086.

Chung, H. L., Little, M., Steinberg, L., & Altschuler, D. (2005). Juvenile Justice and the Transition to adulthood. *Network on Transitions to Adulthood Policy Brief, 20.*

Clark, H.B. (2009). *Practice, Policy, and Research Recommendations on Transition to Adulthood.* National Network on Youth Transition for Behavioral Health.

Clark, H.B., Deschenes, N., Sieler, D., Green, M.E., White, G., & Sondheimer, D.L. (2008). Service for Youth in Transition to Adulthood in Systems of Care. In B.A. Stroul & G.M. Blau (Eds.), *System of care handbook: Transforming mental health services for children, youth, and families* (517-543). Baltimore, Maryland: Brookes Publishing Co.

Clark, H., Mathur, S. R., & Helding, B. (2011). Transition Services for Juvenile Detainees with Disabilities: Findings on Recidivism. *Education & Treatment of Children (West Virginia University Press), 34*(4), 511-529.

Cobb, R. B., & Alwell, M. (2009). Transition Planning/Coordinating Interventions for Youth with Disabilities: A Systematic Review. *Career Development for Exceptional Individuals, 32*(2), 70-81.

Cobb, R. B., Lipscomb, S., Wolgemuth, J., Schulte, T., Veliquette, A., Alwell, M., ... & Welnberg, A. (2013). *Improving Post-High School Outcomes for Transition-Age Students with Disabilities: An Evidence Review* (No. 7877). Washington, DC: Mathematica Policy Research.

Cole, P., & Ferrier, K. (2009). Federal programs and youth workers: Opportunities to Strengthen our Workforce. Next Generation: Youth Work Coalition.

Condon, E., & Callahan, M. (2008). Individualized Career Planning for Students with Significant Support Needs Utilizing the Discovery and Vocational Profile Process, Cross-agency Collaborative Funding and Social Security Work Incentives. *Journal of Vocational Rehabilitation, 28*(2), 85-96.

Davies, P. S., Rupp, K., & Wittenburg, D. (2009). A Life-cycle Perspective on the Transition to Adulthood Among Children Receiving Supplemental Security Income payments. *Journal of Vocational Rehabilitation, 30*(3), 133-151.

Davis, M. (n.d). *Transition to Adulthood.* Presentation.

Davis, M. (2007). *Pioneering transition programs: The Establishment of Programs that Span the Ages Served by Child and Adult Mental Health.* Rockville, MD: Substance Abuse and Mental Health Services Administration, Center for Mental Health Services.

Davis, M., Geller, J.L., & Hunt, B. (2006). Within-state Availability of Transition-to-Adulthood Services for Youths with Serious Mental Health Conditions. *Psychiatric Services 57*(11) 1594-1599. doi: 10.1176/appi. ps.57.11.1594.

Davis, M., Jivanjee, P., & Koroloff, N. (2010). *Paving the way: Meeting Transition Needs of Young People with Developmental Disabilities and Serious Mental Health Conditions.* Portland, OR: Research and Training Center on Family Support and Children's Mental Health.

Davis, M. & Koyanagi, C. (2005). *Summary of Center for Mental Health Services Youth Transition Policy Meeting DRAFT; National experts panel.* Rockville, MD: U.S. Substance Abuse and Mental Health Services Administration, Center for Mental Health Services. Retrieved from www.umassmed.edu/uploadedfiles/ YouthTPM.pdf.

Davis, M. & Sondheimer, D.L. (2005). Child Mental Health Systems' Effort to Support Youth in Transition to Adulthood. *Journal of Behavioral Health Services and Research, 32,* 27-42.

Dion, M.R. (2013). A *Framework for Advancing the Self-sufficiency and Well-being of At-Risk Youth* (OPRE Report # 2012-14). Washington, DC: Office of Planning, Research and Evaluation, Administration for Children and Families, U.S. Department of Health and Human Services.

Elinson, L., Frey, W. D., Li, T., Palan, M. A., & Horne, R. L. (2008). Evaluation of Customized Employment in Building the Capacity of the Workforce Development System. *Journal of Vocational Rehabilitation, 28,* 141-158.

Fabian, E. S. (2007). Urban Youth with Disabilities: Factors Affecting Transition Employment. *Rehabilitation Counseling Bulletin, 50*(3), 130-138.

FamiliesUSA. (n.d.) Long-Term Services Health Reform Provisions: Changes to Medicaid's 1915(i) Option for Home and Community-Based Care. Retrieved from http://www.familiesusa.org/issues/long-term-services/ health-reform/changes-to-medicaids-1915.html.

Fernandes, A. L. (2012). *Vulnerable Youth: Background and Policies.* Congressional Research Service, DIANE Publishing.

Fernandes, A. L., & Gabe, T. (2009). *Disconnected Youth: A Look at 16-to 24-year Olds who are Not Working or in School.* Washington, DC: Congressional Research Service.

Fernandes-Alcantara, A. L. (2012). *Vulnerable youth: Employment and Job Training Programs.* Washington, DC: Congressional Research Service.

Flannery, K. B., Yovanoff, P., Benz, M. R., & Kato, M. M. (2008). Improving Employment Outcomes of Individuals with Disabilities through Short-term Postsecondary Training. *Career Development for Exceptional Individuals, 31*(1), 26-36.

Fleming, A. R., & Fairweather, J. S. (2012). The Role of Postsecondary Education in the Path from High School to Work for Youth with Disabilities. *Rehabilitation Counseling Bulletin, 55*(2), 71-81.

Folk, E. D., Yamamoto, K. K., & Stodden, R. A. (2012). Implementing Inclusion and Collaborative Teaming in a Model Program of Postsecondary Education for Young Adults with Intellectual Disabilities. *Journal of Policy and Practice in Intellectual Disabilities, 9*(4), 257-269.

Fraker, T. (2013). *The Youth Transition Demonstration: Lifting Employment Barriers for Youth with Disabilities.* Washington, DC: Mathematica Policy Research.

Fraker, T., Baird, P., Mamun, A., Manno, M., Martinez, J., & Reed, D. (2012a). *The Social Security Administration's Youth Transition Demonstration Projects: Interim Report on the Career Transition Program.* Washington, DC: Mathematica Policy Research.

Fraker, T., Mamun, A., Manno, M., Martinez, J., Reed, D., & Thompkins, A. (2012b). *The Social Security Administration's Youth Transition Demonstration Projects: Interim report on West Virginia Youth Works* (No. 7639). Washington, DC: Mathematica Policy Research.

Fraker, T., Black, A., Broadus, J., Mamun, A., Manno, M., Martinez, J., ... & Rangarajan, A. (2011a). *The Social Security Administration's Youth Transition Demonstration Projects: Interim report on the City University of New York's Project* (No. 6964). Washington, DC: Mathematica Policy Research.

Fraker, T., Black, A., Mamun, A., Manno, M., Martinez, J., O'Day, B., ... & Rangarajan, A. (2011b). *The Social Security Administration's Youth Transition Demonstration Projects: Interim report on Transition WORKS.* Washington, DC: Mathematica Policy Research.

Fraker, T., Baird, P., Black, A., Mamun, A., Manno, M., Martinez, J., & Rangarajan, A. (2011c). *The Social Security Administration's Youth Transition Demonstration Projects: Interim report on Colorado Youth WINS.* Washington, DC: Mathematica Policy Research.

Gagnon, J. C., & Richards, C. (2008). *Making the Right Turn: A Guide about Improving Transition Outcomes of Youth Involved in the Juvenile Corrections System.* Washington, DC: National Collaborative on Workforce & Disability for Youth, Institute for Educational Leadership. Retrieved from http://www.ncwd-youth.info/assets/juvenile_justice/making_the_right_turn.pdf.

Ganzglass, E. (2010). "New Directions for Workforce Education and Training Policy Require a New Approach to Performance Accountability." Washington, DC: CLASP, Center for Postsecondary and Economic Success.

Gelman, E. & Green, S. (2010). *Independent Evaluation of the Community Mental Health Services Block Grant* (HHS Publication No. SMA 10-4610). Rockville, MD: Center for Mental Health Services, Substance Abuse and Mental Health Services Administration. Retrieved from http://store.samhsa.gov/shin/content/SMA10-4610/SMA10-4610.pdf.

Gonsoulin, S., Darwin, M. J., & Read, N. W. (2012). *Providing Individually Tailored Academic and Behavioral Support Services for Youth in the Juvenile Justice and Child Welfare Systems.* Washington, DC: National Evaluation and Technical Assistance Center for Children and Youth Who Are Neglected, Delinquent, or At-Risk (NDTAC). Retrieved from http://www.neglected-delinquent.org/sites/default/files/docs/NDTAC_PracticeGuide_IndividualSrvcs.pdf

Gonzalez, R., Rosenthal, D. A., & Kim, J. H. (2011). Predicting vocational rehabilitation outcomes of young adults with specific learning disabilities: Transitioning from school to work. *Journal of Vocational Rehabilitation, 34*(3), 163-172.

Green, M., Eigen, B., Lefko, J., & Ebling, S. (2005). Addressing the challenges facing SSA's disability programs. *Social Security Bulletin, 66,* 29.

Griffin, P., Steele, R., & Franklin, K. (2007). Aftercare Reality and Reform. Pennsylvania Progress: A Juvenile Justice Research, Policy, and Practice Series. National Center for Juvenile Justice. Retrieved from http://www.modelsforchange.net/publications/131

Grigal, M., Dwyre, A., & Davis, H. (2006). Transition services for students aged 18-21 with intellectual disabilities in college and community settings: Models and implications of success. *Information Brief, 5*(5), 1-5.

Grigal, M., Hart, D., & Migliore, A. (2011). Comparing the transition planning, postsecondary education, and employment outcomes of students with intellectual and other disabilities. *Career Development for Exceptional Individuals, 34*(1), 4-17.

Grisso, T. (2008). Adolescent Offenders with Mental Disorders. *The Future of Children, 20*(8) pp. 143-164.

Guzman, T., Pirog, M. A., & Seefeldt, K. (2013). Social policy: What have we learned? *Policy Studies Journal, 41*(S1), S53-S70.

Hagner, D., Malloy, J. M., Mazzone, M. W., & Cormier, G. M. (2008). Youth with disabilities in the criminal justice system: Considerations for transition and rehabilitation planning. *Journal of Emotional And Behavioral Disorders, 16*(4), 240-247. doi:10.1177/1063426608316019

Harris, L. (2006). Making the juvenile justice–workforce system connection for re-entering young offenders. Center for Law and Social Policy.

Harris, L., & Bird, K. (2012). Workforce Investment Act Reauthorization may move youth development field back a decade: Analysis of H.R. 4297 through a youth advocacy lens. Washington, DC: CLASP.

Hart, D. (2006). *Research to practice: Postsecondary education options for students with intellectual disabilities.* University of Massachusetts, Boston, Institute for Community Inclusion.

Hartwell, S., Fisher, W., & Davis, M. (2007). Emerging Adults Emerging From Incarceration with Psychiatric Disabilities: Age-Specific Mental Health System Challenges. *Conference Papers - American Sociological Association,* 1.

Hayward, B. J., & Schmidt-Davis, H. (Eds.). (2005). *Longitudinal study of the Vocational Rehabilitation (VR) Services Program, third final report: The context of VR services.* US Department of Education, Office of Special Education and Rehabilitative services, Rehabilitation Services Administration.

Heflinger C.A. & Hoffman C. (2008). Transition Age Youth in Publicly Funded Systems: Identifying High-risk Youth for Policy Planning and Improved Service Delivery. *Journal of Behavioral Health Services & Research.* 35(4):390-401.

Heflinger C.A. & Hoffman C. (2009). Double whammy? Rural Youth with Serious Emotional Disturbance and the Transition to Adulthood. *The Journal of Rural Health: Official Journal of the American Rural Health Association and the National Rural Health Care Association.* 25(4): 399-406. doi:10.1111/j.1748-0361.2009.00251.x.

Hemmeter, J., Kauff, J., & Wittenburg, D. (2009). Changing Circumstances: Experiences of Child SSI Recipients Before and After their Age-18 Redetermination for Adult Benefits. *Journal of Vocational Rehabilitation,30*(3), 201-221.

Hertel-Fernandez, A. (2010). A New Deal for Young Adults: Social Security Benefits for Post-secondary School Students. *Social Security Brief,* 33.

Hoffman, C., Heflinger, C.A., Athay, M. & Davis, M. (2009). Policy, Funding, and Sustainability: Issues and Recommendations for Promoting Effective Transition Systems. In H.B. Clark & D. Unruh (ed.) T*ransition of youth and young adults with emotional or behavioral difficulties: An evidence-based handbook.* Baltimore, Maryland: Brookes Publishing Co.

Honeycutt, T., Thompkins, A., Bardos, M., & Stern, S. (2013). *State Differences in the Vocational Rehabilitation Experiences of Transition-age Youth with Disabilities* (No. 7873). Washington, DC: Mathematica Policy Research.

Honeycutt, T., & Wittenburg, D. (2012). Identifying Transition-age Youth with Disabilities Using Existing Surveys. Washington, DC: Mathematica Policy Research.

Honeycutt, T. (2013). Outcomes of Youth and Young Adults Seeking VR Services. Paper presented at the Disability Research and Policy: New Evidence and Promising Ideas

Jivanlee, P. & Kruzich, J. (2011). Supports for Young People with Mental Health Conditions and Their Families in the Transition Years: Youth and Family Voices. *Best Practices in Mental Health, 7,* 115-133.

Kaufman, B., Lynn, I., Stuart, C., Moone, M., Searcy, L., Rumpel, F.,...Wills, J. (2005). *How Youth with Disabilities are Served through the Workforce Development System: Case Study Research Across Six Sites.* Washington, DC: Academy for Education Development.

Keller-Allen, C. (2006). *English Language learners with Disabilities: Identification and Other State Policies and Issues.* Alexandria, VA: Project Forum, National Association of State Directors of Special Education.

King, L., & Rukh-Kamaa, A. (2013). Note: Youth Transitioning Out of Foster Care: An Evaluation of a Supplemental Security Income Policy Change. *Social Security Bulletin, 73*(3).

Klees, B.S., Wolfe, C.J., & Curtis, C.A. (2011). Medicaid Program Description and Legislative History. Baltimore, MD: Office of the Actuary, Centers for Medicare & Medicaid Services. Retrieved from http://www.ssa.gov/policy/docs/statcomps/supplement/2011/medicaid.html.

Kluss, S. (2012). Juvenile Justice Reform: A Blueprint from the Youth Transition Funders Group. Retrieved from http://www.ytfg.org/documents/Blueprint_JJReform.pdf.

Koball, H., et al. (2011). *Synthesis of Research and Resources to Support At-risk Youth,* OPRE Report # OPRE 2011-22, Washington, DC: Office of Planning, Research and Evaluation, Administration for Children and Families, U.S. Department of Health and Human Services.

Koroloff, N. & Davis, M. (2010). Moving the Field of Transition Services Forward. *Focal Point: Youth, Young Adults, & Mental Health, 24*(1).

Koyanagi, C. & Alfano, E. (2012). P*romise for the Future (Program Factsheets): A Compendium of Fact Sheets on Federal Programs for Transition-Age Youth with Serious Mental Health Conditions.* Washington, DC: Bazelon Center for Mental Health Law. Retrieved from http://www.bazelon.org/News-Publications/Publications/ CategoryID/22/List/1/Level/a/ProductID/66.aspx?SortField=ProductNumberpercent2cProductNumber.

Koyanagi, C., & Alfano, E. (2013). Promise for the Future: How Federal Programs Can Improve Career Outcomes for Youth & Young Adults with Serious Mental Health Conditions. *Psychiatry Information in Brief, 10*(5), 1.

Landmark, L. J., Ju, S., & Zhang, D. (2010). Substantiated Best Practices in Transition: Fifteen Plus Years Later. *Career Development for Exceptional Individuals, 33*(3), 165-176.

Lane, K. L., & Carter, E. W. (2006). Supporting Transition-Age Youth With and At Risk for Emotional and Behavioral Disorders at the Secondary Level: A Need for Further Inquiry. *Journal of Emotional and Behavioral Disorders, 14*(2), 66-70.

Larson, M. (2009). *Supporting Transition to Adulthood Among Youth with Mental Health Needs: Action Steps for Policymakers.* National Collaborative on Workforce & Disability for Youth Policy Brief, 2, 1-10. Retrieved from http://www.ncwd-youth.info/sites/default/files/policybrief-issue-02.pdf.

Leone, P. E., & Weinberg, L. A. (2010). *Addressing the Unmet Educational Needs of Children and Youth in the Juvenile Justice and Child Welfare Systems.* Georgetown University, Center for Juvenile Justice Reform.

Luecking, D.M. (2008). *Sustaining Seamless School to Career Transition. Presentation at the 2008 ICDR/ISE State of the Science Conference.* Retrieved from http://www.seamlesstransition.org/images/stories/media/ISEconfDebraLuecking.ppt.

Lindsay, S. (2011). Employment Status and Work Characteristics Among Adolescents with Disabilities. *Disability and Rehabilitation, 33*(10), 843-854.

Lindstrom, L., Kahn, L. G., & Lindsey, H. (2013). Navigating the Early Career Years: Barriers and Strategies for Young Adults with Disabilities. *Journal of Vocational Rehabilitation, 39*(1), 1-12.

Lipsey, M. W., Howell, J. C., Kelly, M. R., Chapman, G., & Carver, D. (2010). *Improving the Effectiveness of Juvenile Justice Programs.* Washington, DC: Center for Juvenile Justice Reform.

Liu, S., & Stapleton, D. (2011). Longitudinal Statistics on Work Activity and Use of Employment Supports for New Social Security Disability Insurance Beneficiaries. *Social Security Bulletin, 71*(3), 35-59.

Livermore, G. A., Goodman, N., & Wright, D. (2007). Social Security Disability Beneficiaries: Characteristics, Work Activity, and Use of Services. *Journal of Vocational Rehabilitation, 27*(2), 85-93.

Livermore, G., & Stapleton, D. (2010). *Work Activity and Use of Employment Supports Under the Original TTW Regulations report: Highlights of the Fifth Ticket to Work evaluation report.* Washington, DC: Mathematica Policy Research.

Luecking, D. M., & Luecking, R. G. (2013). Translating Research into a Seamless Transition Model. *Career Development and Transition for Exceptional Individuals,* 2165143413508978.

Luecking, R. G., & Wittenburg, D. (2009). Providing Supports to Youth with Disabilities Transitioning to Adulthood: Case Descriptions from the Youth Transition Demonstration. *Journal of Vocational Rehabilitation, 30*(3), 241-251.

Lynn, I., & Mack, D. (2008). *Improving Transition Outcomes of Youth with Disabilities by Increasing Access to Apprenticeship Opportunities.* ODEP Issue Papers Project. Retrieved from http://www.dol.gov/odep/categories/youth/apprenticeship/ApprenticeshipIssuePaper.pdf.

Madaus, J. W., & Shaw, S. F. (2006). The Impact of the IDEA 2004 on Transition to College for Students with Learning Disabilities. *Learning Disabilities Research & Practice, 21*(4), 273-281.

Mallett, C. (2009). Disparate Juvenile Court Outcomes for Disabled Delinquent Youth: A Social Work Call to Action. *Child & Adolescent Social Work Journal, 26*(3), 197-207.

Mann, C. & Hyde, P.S. (2013). *Joint CMCS and SAMHSA Informational Bulletin: Coverage of Behavioral Health Services for Children, Youth, and Young Adults with Significant Mental Health Conditions.* Baltimore, MD: Centers for Medicare & Medicaid Services. Retrieved from http://medicaid.gov/Federal-Policy-Guidance/Downloads/CIB-05-07-2013.pdf.

Mann, D. R., & Wittenburg. (2012). *Back to Work: Recent SSA Employment Demonstrations for People with Disabilities.* Center for Studying Disability Policy. Washington, DC: Mathematica Policy Research. Retrieved from http://www.mathematica-mpr.com/publications/pdfs/disability/backtowork_ib.pdf.

Manteuffel, B., Stephens, R.L., Sondheimer, D.L., & Fisher, S.K. (2008). Characteristics, Service Experiences, and Outcomes of Transition-Aged Youth in Systems of Care: Policy Implications. *Journal of Behavioral Health Services & Research.* 35(4):469–487. doi:10.0007/s11414-008-9130-6.

Martinez, J., Fraker, T., Manno, M., Baird, P., Mamun, A., O'Day, B., ... & Wittenburg, D. (2010). *The Social Security Administration's Youth Transition Demonstration Projects: Implementation Lessons from the Original Projects.* Washington, DC: Mathematica Policy Research.

Moreno, L., Honeycutt, T., McLeod, S., & Gill, C. (2013). *Lessons for Programs Serving Transition-Age Youth: A Comparative Analysis of the US and 10 Other Countries in the Organisation for Economic Co-Operation and Development (OECD)* (No. 7766). Washington, DC: Mathematica Policy Research.

Morris, J. A., Day, S., & Schoenwald, S. K. (2010). *Turning Knowledge Into Practice: A Manual for Human Service Administrators and Practitioners About Understanding and Implementing Evidence-Based Practices, second edition (revised).* Boston: The Technical Assistance Collaborative, Inc.

Muller, E. (2010). *State Longitudinal Data Systems for Tracking Outcomes for Students with Disabilities Through Postsecondary activities.* Alexandria, VA: Project Forum.

Muller, E. (2011). *Reentry Programs for Students with Disabilities in the Juvenile Justice System: Four State Approaches.* inForum: Brief Policy Analysis.

Muller, E., & Burdette, P. (2007). *Highly Qualified Teachers and Special Education: Several State Approaches.* Alexandria, VA: Project Forum.

NASMHPD Research Institute, Inc. (2007). *How State Mental Health Agencies Use the Community Mental Health Services Block Grant to Improve Care and Transform Systems: 2007.* Retrieved from http://www.healthcare.uiowa.edu/icmh/documents/MHBGReportSection508-5-6-08.pdf.

NASMHPD Research Institute, Inc. (2012). *FY2010 State Mental Health Revenues and Expenditures.* Retrieved from http://www.nri-inc.org/reports_pubs/2012/RESummary2010.pdf.

National Center for Education Statistics, Institute of Education Sciences, U.S. Department of Education. (2012). Table 118. Number of 14- through 21-year-old students served under Individuals with Disabilities Education Act, Part B, who exited school, by exit reason, age, and type of disability: 2007-08 and 2008-09. Digest of Education Statistics: 2011 (NCES 2012-001). Retrieved from http://nces.ed.gov/programs/digest/d11/tables/dt11_118.asp.

National Center on Workforce & Disability (n.d.). *One-Stops: Getting Involved in transition.* Boston, MA: National Center on Workforce & Disability. Retrieved from http://www.onestops.info/article.php?article_id=82#idea.

National Collaborative on Workforce & Disability for Youth. (2013). *Disability legislation – All Acts.* Washington, DC: Author. Retrieved from http://www.ncwd-youth.info/legislation/all#acw.

National Collaborative on Workforce & Disability for Youth. (2008). P*erformance Data and Youth with Disabilities (Workforce Investment Act).* Washington, DC: Author.

National Collaborative on Workforce & Disability for Youth. (2009). Successful Transition Models for Youth with Mental Health Needs: A Guide for Workforce Professionals. *InfoBrief (23).* Retrieved from http://www.ncwd-youth.info/information-brief-23.

National Collaborative on Workforce & Disability for Youth. (2010). Improving Transition Outcomes for Youth Involved in the Juvenile Justice System: Practical Considerations. *InfoBrief (25).* Retrieved from http://www.ncwd-youth.info/sites/default/files/Improving_Outcomes_for_Youth_Involved_in_Juvenile_Justice.pdf

National Collaborative on Workforce & Disability for Youth. (2012). Developing a Professional Development System for Youth Service Professionals. *InfoBrief (35).* Retrieved from http://www.ncwd-youth.info/sites/default/files/infobrief-35-credentialing-brief.pdf.

National Collaborative on Workforce & Disability for Youth and Workforce Strategy Center. (2009). *Career-Focused Services for Students with Disabilities at Community Colleges.* Washington, D.C.: Institute for Educational Leadership. Retrieved from http://www.ncwd-youth.info/assets/background/disabilities-and-community-colleges.pdf.

National Council on Disability. (2008). "The Rehabilitation Act: Outcomes for Transition-Age Youth. Washington, DC: National Council on Disability. Retrieved from: http://www.ncd.gov/publications/2008/10282008.

National Disability Rights Network. (2012). Juvenile Justice. *National Disability Rights Network.* Retrieved from http://www.ndrn.org/en/issues/juvenile-justice.html.

National Institute of Mental Health. (2013). *Important Events in NIMH History.* Retrieved from http://www.nih.gov/about/almanac/organization/NIMH.htm.

Ne'eman, A. (2012). *The Affordable Care Act and the I/DD community: An Overview of the Law and Advocacy Priorities Going Forward.* Washington, DC: Autistic Self Advocacy Network. Retrieved from http://autisticadvocacy.org/wp-content/uploads/2013/09/ACA-ASAN-policy-brief.pdf.

Nelson, C.M., Jolivette, K., Leone, P.E., & Mathur, S.R. (2010). Meeting the Needs of At-Risk and Adjudicated Youth with Behavioral Challenges: The Promise of Juvenile Justice. *Behavioral Disorders, 36*(1) pp. 70-80.

Neubert, D. A., & Moon, M. S. (2006). Postsecondary Settings and Transition Services for Students with Intellectual Disabilities: Models and Research. *Focus on Exceptional Children, 39*(4), 1.

Newman, L., Wagner, M., Knokey, A. M., Marder, C., Nagle, K., Shaver, D., & Wei, X. (2011). T*he Post-High School Outcomes of Young Adults with Disabilities Up to 8 years After High School: A Report from the National Longitudinal Transition Study-2 (NLTS-2).* NCSER 2011-3005. Washington, DC: National Center for Special Education Research.

Nuñez-Neto, B. (2007). *Juvenile Justice: Overview of Legislative History and Funding Trends (CRS Report No. 22070).* Washington, DC: Congressional Research Service. Retrieved from http://assets.opencrs.com/rpts/RS22070_20070125.pdf.

Office of Disability Employment Policy. (2013). *Healthy Transitions: A Pathway to Employment for Youth with Chronic Health Conditions and Other Disabilities.* Retrieved from http://www.dol.gov/odep/pdf/2013ODEPHealthyReport.pdf.

Office of Special Education Programs, U.S. Department of Education. (2007). *IDEA Regulations: Secondary Transition.* Retrieved from http://idea.ed.gov/explore/view/p/,root,dynamic,TopicalBrief,17.

O'Day, B. (2012). *Youth Perspectives on the Transition to Adulthood.* Presentation at the Future for Young Americans with Disabilities: Economic Success or Dependence?

O'Day, B., & Stapleton, D. (2009). *Transforming Disability Policy for Youth and Young Adults with Disabilities.* Disability Policy Research Brief. Washington, DC: Mathematica Policy Research.

O'Leary, P., Livermore, G. A., & Stapleton, D. C. (2011). Employment of Individuals in the Social Security Disability Programs. *Social Security Bulletin, 71,* 1.

Osgood, D., Foster, E., & Courtney, M. E. (2010). Vulnerable Populations and the Transition to Adulthood. *Future of Children, 20*(1), 209-229.

Plotner, A.J., Trach, J.S., & Strauser, D.R. (2012). Vocational Rehabilitation Counselors' Identified Transition Competencies: Perceived Importance, Frequency, and Preparedness. *Rehabilitation Counseling Bulletin, 55* (3), 135-143.

Podmostko, M. (2007). Tunnels and Cliffs: A Guide for Workforce Development Practitioners and Policymakers Serving Youth with Mental Health Needs. Washington, DC: National Collaborative on Workforce & Disability for Youth. *Institute for Educational Leadership.*

Poisal, K. & Cooper, R. (n.d.) 1915(i) *State Plan Home and Community-Based Services (HCBS).* Division of Long Term Services and Supports, Disabled and Elderly Health Programs Group, Center for Medicaid, CHIP, and Survey and Certification, Center for Medicare and Medicaid Services.

Pottick, K.J., Bilder, S., Stoep, A.V., Warner, L.A., & Alvarez, M.F. (2008). US Patterns of Mental Health Service Utilization for Transition-Age Youth and Young Adults. *The Journal of Behavioral Health Services and Research, 35,* 373-388.

Povenmire-Kirk, T. C., Lindstrom, L., & Bullis, M. (2010). De Escuela a la Vida Adulta/From School to Adult Life: Transition Needs for Latino Youth with Disabilities and Their Families. *Career Development for Exceptional Individuals, 33*(1), 41-51.

Pullmann, M.D., Heflinger, C.A., & Mayberry, L.S. (2010). Patterns of Medicaid Disenrollment for Youth with Mental Health Problems. *Medical Care Research and Review, 67,* 657-675.

Rhodes, G. (2010). *Vocational Rehabilitation (VR) Research in Brief: A Partnership in Career Development for People with Disabilities: Collaboration Between Vocational Rehabilitation Counselors and Families.* Washington, DC: US Department of Education.

Shandra, C. L., & Hogan, D. P. (2008). School-to-Work Program Participation and the Post-High School Employment of Young Adults with Disabilities. *Journal of Vocational Rehabilitation, 29*(2), 117-130.

Shaw, S. F., Madaus, J. W., & Banerjee, M. (2009). Enhance Access to Postsecondary Education for Students with Disabilities. *Intervention in School and Clinic, 44*(3), 185-190.

Sheedy, C. K. & Whitter, M. *Guiding Principles and Elements of Recovery-Oriented Systems of Care: What Do We Know from the Research? (HHS Publication No. SMA 09-4439).* Rockville, MD: Center for Substance Abuse Treatment, Substance Abuse, and Mental Health Services Administration, 2009.

Sheldon, J. R., & Lopez-Soto, E. J. (2009). Plan for Achieving Self-Support. An SSI Work Incentive and Approach to Self-Directing Vocational Rehabilitation to Support a Range of Work Goals. NY Makes Work Pay Policy to Practice Brief# 1. *Employment and Disability Institute Collection, 1267.*

Social Security Administration. (2013a). *Monthly Statistical Snapshot, August 2013.* Washington, DC: Social Security Administration. Retrieved from http://www.ssa.gov/policy/docs/quickfacts/stat_snapshot/.

Social Security Administration. (2013b). *Spotlight on Plans To Achieve Self-Support – 2013 edition.* Washington, DC: Social Security Administration. Retrieved from http://www.socialsecurity.gov/ssi/spotlights/spot-plans-self-support.htm.

Social Security Administration. (2013c). *Ticket to Work: Choosing a Service Provider that is Right for You.* Work Incentives Seminar Event, June 26, 2013. Retrieved from http://www.ilr.cornell.edu/edi/media/WISE/2013-06-26/2013-06-26_WISE_Webinar.pdf.

Social Security Administration. (2013d). *Spotlight on Student Earned Income Exclusion – 2013 edition.* Washington, DC: Social Security Administration. Retrieved from http://www.ssa.gov/ssi/spotlights/spot-student-earned-income.htm.

Social Security Administration. (2012). Annual Statistical report on the Social Security Disability Insurance program, 2011. Baltimore, MD: Office of Retirement and Disability Policy.

Sopko, K. M. (2009). Universal Design for Learning: Policy Challenges and Recommendations. Project Forum. National Association of State Directors of Special Education.

Smith, F. A., Grigal, M., Sulewsi, J. (2012). *Postsecondary Education and Employment Outcomes for Aransition-Age Youth with and without Disabilities: A Secondary Analysis of American Community Survey Data.* Boston, MA: University of Massachusetts Boston, Institute for Community Inclusion.

Stapleton, D., Mamun, A., & Page, J. (2013). *Initial impacts of the Ticket to Work Program for Young New Social Security Disability Awardees: Estimates Based on Randomly Assigned Mail Months* (No. 7881). Mathematica Policy Research.

Stenhjem, P. (2005). Youth with Disabilities in the Juvenile Justice System: Prevention and Intervention Strategies. *Examining Current Challenges in Secondary Education and Transition: Issue Brief, 4*(1).

Stewart, D., Freeman, M., Law, M., Healy, H., Burke-Gaffney, J., Forhan, M., ... & Guenther, S. (2010). Transition to adulthood for youth with disabilities: Evidence from the literature. *International Encyclopedia of Rehabilitation.*

Sturgis, C. (2013). Eduployment: Creating Opportunity Policies for America's Youth. Youth Transition Funders Group. Retrieved from http://www.ytfg.org/documents/eduployment.pdf.

Substance Abuse and Mental Health Services Administration, HHS Publication No. SMA-13-4756. (2013). *Promoting recovery and independence for older adolescents and young adults.* Washington, D.C.: Author.

Technical Assistance Partnership for Child and Family Mental Health. (n.d.) *Introduction to Systems of Care.* Retrieved from http://www.tapartnership.org/SOC/SOCintro.php.

Test, D. W., Mazzotti, V. L., Mustian, A. L., Fowler, C. H., Kortering, L., & Kohler, P. (2009). Evidence-Based Secondary Transition Predictors for Improving Postschool Outcomes for Students with Disabilities. *Career Development for Exceptional Individuals, 32*(3), 160-181.

Thakur, M. (2012). *Response to Request for Information on Strategies for Improving Outcomes for Disconnected Youth.* Washington, DC: National Youth Employment Council.

Ticket to Work and Work Incentives Advisory Panel. (2007). *Building on the Ticket: A New Paradigm for Investing in Economic Self-Sufficiency for People with Significant Disabilities.* Final Report to the President and Congress, Year Eight of the Panel.

Trainor, A. A. (2010). Adolescents with Disabilities Transitioning to Adulthood: Implications for a Diverse and Multicultural Population. *The Prevention Researcher, 17*(1), 12-16.

Trainor, A. A., Lindstrom, L., Simon-Burroughs, M., Martin, J. E., & Sorrells, A. M. (2008). From Marginalized to Maximized: Opportunities for Diverse Youths with Disabilities: A Position Paper of the Division on Career Development and Transition. *Career Development for Exceptional Individuals, 31*(1), 56-64.

The Study Group. (2007). "An Assessment of Transition Policies and Practices in State Vocational Rehabilitation Agencies." Kill Devil Hills, NC: The Study Group, Inc.

Thornton, C., Livermore, G., Fraker, T., Stapleton, D., O'Day, B., Wittenburg, D., ... & Mamun, A. (2007). *Evaluation of the Ticket to Work Program: Assessment of Post-Rollout Implementation and Early Impacts, volume 1.* Washington, DC: Mathematica Policy Research.

Unruh, D., Povenmire-Kirk, T., & Yamamoto, S. (2009). Perceived Barriers and Protective Factors of Juvenile Offenders on their Developmental Pathway to Adulthood. *Journal Of Correctional Education, 60*(3), 201-224.

Unruh, D.K., Waintrap, M.G., Canter, T., & Smith, S. (2009). Improving Transition Outcomes of Young Offenders. In *Transition of Youth and Young Adults with Emotional or Behavioral Difficulties: An Evidence-Supported Handbook.* (Hewitt B. Clark & Deanne K. Unruh, Eds.) Baltimore, Maryland: Paul H. Brooks Publishing Co.

U.S. Department of Education. (2006). *Title I, Part D: Neglected, Delinquent, and At-Risk Youth Prevention and Intervention Programs for Children and Youth Who Are Neglected, Delinquent, or At-Risk (N Or D): Nonregulatory Guidance.* Retrieved from http://www2.ed.gov/policy/elsec/guid/nord.doc.

U.S. Department of Education. (2013) *The Rehabilitation Act.* Retrieved from http://www2.ed.gov/policy/speced/reg/narrative.html.

U.S. Department of Education. (2013) *Vocational Rehabilitation State Grants.* Retrieved from http://www2.ed.gov/programs/rsabvrs/index.html.

U.S. Department of Labor. (2013). *Workforce System Results.* Washington, DC: US Department of Labor. Retrieved from: http://www.doleta.gov/performance/results/pdf/workforceSystemResultsJune2013.pdf.

U.S. Government Accountability Office. (2008). *Federal Action Could Address Some of the Challenges Faced by Local Programs that Reconnect Youth to Education and Employment.* Washington, DC.

U.S. Government Accountability Office, Report 08-313. (2008a). *Disconnected Youth: Federal Action Could Address Some of the Challenges Faced by Local Programs That Reconnect Youth to Education and Employment.* Retrieved from http://www.gao.gov/new.items/d08313.pdf.

U.S. Government Accountability Office, Report 08-678 (2008b). *Young Adults with Serious Mental Illness: Some States and Federal Agencies are Taking Steps to Address their Transition Challenges.* Washington, D.C. Retrieved from http://www.gao.gov/assets/280/277167.pdf.

Walters, D., Zanghi, M., Ansell, D., Armstrong, E., & Sutter, K. (2011). *Transition Planning with Adolescents: A Review of Principles and Practices Across Systems.* Tulsa, OK: National Resource Center for Youth Development and the University of Southern Maine.

Wagner, J.O., Sturko Grossman, C.R., Wonacott, M.E., & Jackson, D. (2007). Focused Futures Youth Development System Builder: Elements of a WIA Youth Program. Ohio State University.

Weir, C., Grigal, M., Hart, D. & Boyle, M. (2013) *Profiles and Promising Practices in Higher Education for Students with Intellectual Disability.* Think College. Boston, MA: University of Massachusetts Boston, Institute for Community Inclusion.

Williams, B. & Tolbert, J. (2007). *Aging out of EPSDT: Issues for Young Adults with Disabilities.* Washington, DC: The henry J. Kaiser Family Foundation.

Woolsey, L., & Katz-Leavy, J. (2008). *Transitioning Youth with Mental Health Needs to Meaningful Employment and Independent Living.* National Collaborative on Workforce & Disability for Youth, Institute for Educational Leadership. Retrieved from http://www.ncwd-youth.info/assets/reports/mental_health_case_study_report.pdf.